Unflappable

THE LIFE AND TIMES OF WHITNEY REED

by C F Stewart

UNFLAPPABLE: THE LIFE, LOVES, AND TIMES OF WHITNEY REED
By C.F. Stewart

Published by Sorento Publishing
41470 Kansas Street
Palm Desert, CA 92211 USA
760 360-5586
court@easytouseeasytowin.com
www.easytowineasytouse.com

Cover & Book Design: Solomon Faber - Solomon's Design Studio

Edited by: The world renown racehorse sports columnist Larry Stumes, freelance writer extraordinaire.

ISBN: 0-9749023-2-2

Dedication:
I wish to dedicate this book to my parents Annie and Rollie Reed, my sister Susan Kircher, and most importantly, my son Whitney R. Reed Jr. Next time around I'll win Wimbledon for all of you.

Inspiration is like sunny weather in Alameda, you never know when it's going to make an appearance.

With special thanks to:
CFS, Jack & Helenka Frost, Bud Collins, Dennis Hennessee, Ed Atkinson, Claudia Reed, Jackie Cooper, Jack Darrah, Ken Sheffield, Dick Underhill, Joanna Reed, Jim Nelson, Dan Dillon, Ray Stewart, Frank Geisler, Bob Hill. John Henry, Tom Witteman, Debra K. Harrison, Steve Harman, Donna Gilmore. Much appreciation to my agent, business manager, Gail Feaster.

Table of Contents

- CHAPTER 1 -

In The Beginning

Some folks feel that if you are charming and witty, and live life with verve and imagination, God will cut you some slack. Some folks feel that if you keep God amused enough, he may ignore a few shortcomings and allow the tiniest of indiscretions. Maybe even let you get away with a little sin here and there. Whitney didn't conscientiously elect to play flim-flam with the Lord; Whitney was playing Whitney, and God must have thought it was a hoot, because Whitney Reed, at 74, has a little trouble breathing, but he still looks good; he can still hold a racquet, and he still perks up when an attractive woman walks by.

Whitney was born August 20, 1932 in Oakland, California. The family moved to Alameda when he was four. His father was a jet mechanic at the Naval Air Station in Alameda; his mother was a nurse, homemaker, and tennis player. Friends say the homemaker, nurse, and tennis player may not have been the exact order of importance.

The 1930s were not the best of times. The country was still in the depths of the Great Depression. Nazism was on the rise in Germany, and war in Europe was only a few years off. Considering the difficult times the '30s represented, Whitney's parents were ahead of the mean. They both had jobs. They had a small but comfortable home, and no one in the family missed a meal. Whitney didn't walk to school in a foot of snow with sodden tennis shoes on his feet. He didn't sell newspapers or apples on the street corners, and his father didn't get drunk and beat him up for a little extra exercise.

It is safe to say, Whitney had a very conventional childhood. He didn't fight his way out of the ghetto to become one of the best tennis players in the world. He didn't face racial inequality, segregation, and school busing to finally reach the hollowed ground of Wimbledon. He was a skinny little blond kid who lived in a quaint little town with malt shops, sock hops, and hot apple pie. He walked to school down Sycamore lined streets, and played Pirates of the Caribbean in the estuary. Nothing he did growing up would indicate that he was destined to live a life as eccentric and unconventional as any athlete in recent memory, and nothing he did growing up would indicate that he was destined to become one of the unique characters in sports history.

A word of warning, read the following text with the understanding that it was written in the same manner as Whitney lived his life: seemingly without direction, seemingly without continuity, and seemingly without deliberation.

Whitney was probably lucky that country clubs, exclusive tennis clubs, and expensive coaches did not make an appearance in his early life. These trappings may have influenced him in an adverse way. Coaches, especially, would have found his unique style daunting. They would see the talent and attempt to mold it in a traditional sense. The effort would have been as successful as trying to mold Janis Joplin into Beverly Sills.

During the formative years, from diapers to post puberty, Whitney and his parents would pile into the family car and head for Washington Park tennis courts in Alameda. The court protocol was simple: You win, you stay on the court; you lose, and it can be hours before you play again. Even as a kid, Whitney hated to lose and he hated to sit around waiting for a court. Accordingly, he'd do everything possible to hold the court. Not an easy task when you are young, scrawny, and diminutive. So instead of swinging as hard as his skinny little arms would allow, he became very crafty. He learned to drop-shot, lob, and slice his forehand and backhand. Since running was not something he enjoyed if there was an easier way, the center of the court became his domain. Fifty years later, the center of the court is still his domain.

Playing tournaments tennis began early for Whitney, somewhere between the womb and 12 years old. The Oakland Post Enquirer sponsored a public playground tournament. All the playgrounds in the area sent their best kids. The first year Whitney lost in an early round. He went back to Alameda and began practicing against his garage door. He spent hours hitting forehands and backhands until either his father or the neighbors called a halt to the incessant banging. The distance from the garage door to the gutter is almost the same as the net to the service line – coincidence? The next year he won the playground tournament.

From 13 to 15 he played all the sanctioned junior tournaments, winning most of them in Northern California. At age 15 he went east to Kalamazoo, Mich., for the national 15 and under. Whitney lost to Allen Cleveland in the semifinals. Two years later in Kalamazoo he played Ham Richardson in the finals of the juniors and lost in a very contested match. Whitney got a measure of retribution in doubles; he and Norm Peterson beat Jack Frost and Richardson in the finals. The Richardson/Frost win was huge. Ham Richardson went on to win two NCAA tennis titles. He was ranked number one in the U.S. in 1956 and then again in 1958. He played on seven Davis Cup teams, compiling a record of 20-2. The doubles final in Kalamazoo was a pretty good win for a couple of skinny blond kids from Alameda.

- CHAPTER 2 -

Next Stop,
Alameda High School

If you possess incredible hand-eye coordination, are reasonably fleet of foot, and consider the team concept about as appealing as geometry, you need to think tennis. Whitney probably considered tennis, because if he didn't, as a little tike, he would have spent a lot of time home alone, and he had no fondness for geometry.

Whether his parents had to wake him every Saturday morning and drag him kicking and screaming to the tennis court is conjecture. Whether they made him leave his homework and bat a tennis ball against the garage door is also conjecture. However it occurred, Whitney would say he "got real good at tennis." So good that no one wanted to play the kid from Alameda who never missed a shot.

How Alameda kids "got good at tennis" is a mystery. There was no coaching in a true sense. If a kid was looking to play tennis, he needed to wait at a playground for someone to come along toting a tennis racquet. Sometimes the kids set up matches at the various playgrounds – sort of, like an Old West shootout. Two players would meet at Washington Park, the winner would enhance his reputation, and the loser would look to tomorrow for redemption. Rarely, a more accomplished older player, maybe 18, would help a younger kid with a serve or ground strokes. For Whitney, it wasn't long before the competition petered out completely. Not even the 18-year-olds wanted to play the little kid who strolled around the middle of the court hitting the ball where no one could return it.

High School tennis was a big disappointment both competitively and socially. Whitney had to hide his racquet somewhere along Santa Clara Avenue on his way to school. Kids who carried tennis racquets didn't get the best seat at the malt shops. The kids who carried tennis racquets didn't get the prettiest coeds. Tennis must have satisfied a deep need in young Whitney, because he played at the risk of compromising social situations that are very important to maturing teenagers with delicate psyches.

There were a few crowning moments in Whitney's high school tennis career. He and Norm Peterson won the National Junior Doubles in 1950, and Whitney beat Jack Darrah about 1000 times in high school matches. Later in life Darrah enjoyed a modicum of retribution, he won about a zillion dollars from Whitney playing backgammon.

- CHAPTER 3 -

Next Stop, University of Southern California

Wild ones don't do well in a university setting unless they have an IQ of 150 or more. Whitney is very bright but his IQ is a little shy of 150. So when a bunch of Sigma Nu brothers captured him, made him imbibe strong drink, and then left him at the beach in the company of the ubiquitous blond blue-eyed Delta Gama, his university life was destined to be short-lived. Think about it, Whitney went to USC to play tennis and have fun. Who can have fun, play tennis, and compete academically at the university level? Not any one I know, not unless you have the constitution of a Bill Clinton. Consequently, after a year in the warm Southern California sun, Whitney returned to Alameda.

- CHAPTER 4 -

Next Stop,
Modesto Junior College

Fred Earle, the school's tennis coach, fashioned a legendary array of talent in the '50s and '60s. Whitney was, for awhile, the perfect addition to Earle's parade of stars. The team was so strong in 1951, the little junior college from the valley beat USC and UCLA on consecutive days. Whitney, Jerry DeWitt, and Norm Peterson crushed the best players in the Pacif Eight Conference. However, as Art Larsen before him, Whitney did not mesh with the mold created by Coach Earle.

Whitney, for the second time, was not ready for the discipline of college life. Ironically, it was not because of the plethora of distractions, but because of the lack of distractions. In the summer, an energetic young man could visit all the hotspots, chase all the good-looking farm girls, and be back on campus before the sun set. For Whitney, boredom was worse than the sin of gluttony; consequently, the lack of action, the surfeit of overweight coed agriculture majors, and the tolerance of coach Earle terminated Whitney's second stint in the pursuit of a higher education.

- CHAPTER 5 -

Air Force and
The Korean War

Whitney joined the Air Force in 1952, when men entered the military for a myriad of reasons. It could have been court-ordered, or to find a new life, or to avoid a hostile husband or father. In Whitney's case it was the latter. He unfortunately had formed a relationship with the daughter of a well-known tennis coach whose ideas conflicted with his own as to whom his daughter picked for a playmate. As far as Whitney was concerned, the relationship was standard operating procedure, but from the coach's prospective it was get out of town and don't come back. The well-known coach hustled Whitney into his car, drove him back to Alameda, and deposited him on his parents' front porch. The coach told his father that Whitney was almost as incorrigible as Art Larsen.

Whitney's dad said, "Let's go for a ride, son."

In front of the Air Force recruiting office, Whitney and his dad stopped at a red light. When the light turned green Whitney said, "The light's green dad."

Whitney's dad said, "I know son. This is as far as you go."

Consequently, Whitney bid a tearful goodbye to the daughter, his parents, and the well-known coach and joined the Air Force for a four-year gig.

Four years in the Air Force went by fast. Tennis with a general in Tokyo and a short stint in Korea were pretty much the highlights. No shootings, no bombings, maybe a little dysentery and jock itch, but for the most part Whitney was out of harm's way. Too bad that couldn't be said for the Air Force, for Whitney's style was never in sync with the traditional position of the military. So far out of sync that one adventurous 2nd lieutenant threatened to have Whitney arrested and tried for desertion.

It was in the demilitarized zone during the peace talks; Whitney was supposed to monitor phones and relay any pertinent information. Every day at 6 a.m., a bus would pick up Whitney and deposit his replacement. One afternoon, with a big softball game in the offing, the bus came and there was no replacement. From Whitney's perspective, the Air Force screwed up. They forgot his replacement. Consequently, Whitney grabbed his gear and jumped on the bus.

He reached the baseball field, just in time to throw the first pitch. The first batter hit a comeback grounder that Whitney fielded cleanly. He spun and threw to first. As his eye followed the ball into the mitt of the first baseman, he realized that the first baseman was, in fact, his replacement. As his eye focused a little farther, two very large MPs came into view. One of the MPs motioned for Whitney and his replacement to stand at attention. Whitney and his replacement were placed in handcuffs, and escorted to an area in the stockade reserved for the most serious of crimes – crimes that carry the death penalty.

Fortunately, for Whitney, he was not shot, and neither was his replacement. They lost a couple of stripes, and endured the humiliation of extra kitchen duty. An officer, who was not a tennis player, felt a more appropriate punishment would be somewhere between the rack and the guillotine. Whitney's relationship with a general in Tokyo helped obviate the situation. The general couldn't have his doubles partner shot, not with the annual service tennis tournament in the offing.

.

- CHAPTER 6 -

San Jose State
1958 to 1959

Every university on the planet has at least one individual who remembers everything. That person remembers the names and measurements of all the good-looking sorority girls. That person remembers all beer busts, all the football games, and the girls who were willing and who were not. This individual knows everybody. They know the year of the high school and college graduation of every living soul they ever encountered.

At San Jose State in 1958, there were several of those all-knowing individuals. John Henry and Dick Underhill are two of the more colorful. Both men are bartenders, and both are endowed with elephant-type memories.

If a person walked into the bar at Peacock Gap and asked John Henry who was the starting inside linebacker on the 1958 San Jose State varsity football team he'd respond, "Dick Erler, Washington High '56, big kid, ran like an antelope." If someone asked John who Whitney Reed was, he'd respond, "Tennis player, Alameda High '48, great touch, skinny little kid."

A word to the wise: If you don't want to have a great time spending the afternoon listening to Bay Area athletic lore, you'd better be on your way fast.

Dick Underhill is a little younger, talks almost as fast, and is as knowledgeable as John Henry. The only real difference is size. Dick is about 6'-0"; John is about 6'-4".

I called Dick to get a feel for Whitney's San Jose college days. I expected the usual repartee – good guy, great tennis player, could have been the best ever. I got the usual repartee and considerably more. Dick said he could get in touch with a mutual friend, and set up a rendezvous for some Whitney Reed lore. We decided that Starbucks on Van Ness in the city would be the most convenient.

I figured the best way to make things work out for everyone was to pick up Whitney in Alameda, cross the bridge, drop Whitney in front of Starbucks, and find a parking spot. We were a little late, but everything else fell into place. Five minutes after I dropped Whitney off, we were in Starbucks, standing in front of a very attractive woman, who announced that she was a student from Israel.

Dick introduced me to Ken Sheffield. Whitney hugged Ken like a long-lost brother. No one introduced the Israeli student. I know how old Whitney is and I can guess how old Dick and Ken are, so what's with the 25-year-old Israeli student? After conjuring up all kinds of lurid scenarios, I realized we intruded on the poor girl's table.

Dick and I were on one side of the table, and Whitney and Ken were on the other side. The Israeli student was reading a book at the head of the table.

Ken and Whitney launched into some major reminiscing while I frantically reach for recorders and notepaper.

When you are in your mid-60s and early-70s, reminiscing about college life is as good as it gets. Great athletic feats are more dramatic, and the parties are more spectacular. The memories morph into a collage of faces, bodies, and sensuous moments. Times like reminiscing at Starbachs make getting old not so much of a bitch.

Ken Sheffield is to storytelling as O'Henry is to short story writing. He's animated, and his voice changes as the characters in his story play out their parts. He mimics Whitney's unique voice as well as anyone, which makes the stories so real it's scary.

Ken's version of the 1963 Canadian Nationals is as funny a story as any gag writer could conjure up, and Ken's story is true.

Whitney was in desperate need of a ride to Vancouver, and Ken had just taken a job selling Shick razors on the road. It doesn't take a New York drama critic to guess the ensuing plot. Ken figures he can sell Shick razors in Canada as well as any-where, and traveling with Whitney may not be the safest health plan, but it's bound to be fun. They stock up an ample supply of premium beer and head up Highway 101 for Vancouver.

An ample supply of beer was defined by how much they could consume in a 200-mile period. The ride to Canada in 1963 was somewhat of a blur. Somewhere along the way, Whitney called home to tell everyone that he was in transit to Canada, alive and well. Whitney's mom says great, thanks for calling, and Tom Brown can't play doubles.

Tom Brown and Whitney are the No. 1-seeded doubles team. With Tom not playing, Whitney needed to find a new partner. He looked over at Ken.

They made Vancouver in one piece. First on the agenda was to convince the Canadian National tournament committee that Ken was qualified to play in their National tournament. Whitney fabricated this wonderful resume for Sheffield. Ken was unbeaten in his last 20 hardcourt matches, and he left out the fact that the hardcourt matches were played in Penngrove, California. Further, Ken was the No. 1 player in his area, and he left out the fact that the area was Cotati, California. This was before the Internet, so the organizing committee couldn't go on line and verify the real Ken Sheffield. Because Whitney was very popular in Canada, the organizing committee had lit-tle choice – Ken was in the tournament. Not only in the tour-nament, but Ken and Whitney were still the No. 1 seed.

Being seeded first had its advantages; they wouldn't have to play the No. 2 seed in the first round. A problem that was not easily ameliorated was the surface. Ken had never played on grass.

Whitney told Ken that playing on grass was no biggie; you just needed to bend your knees a little more. He told Ken that the ball didn't bounce very high, and that made dinks pretty effective. By this time, Ken was feeling that he should have stayed in San Francisco. He and Whitney had been in some tight spots, but never was he put in a situation were he could suffer some major humiliation. Participating in an international tennis event on a foreign surface with one of the best players in the world had humiliation written all over it.

The score of the first-round match after all these years is irrelevant – no one remembers and no one cares – but two incidents occurred that are indelibly etched on Ken Sheffield's brain.

The first serve in the first set was incident No. 1 – the ball skidded off the grass and Sheffield's racquet flew out of his hand. Incident No. 2 caused Ken to consider therapy. After chasing all those skidding low balls all over the court, he finally got his chance for a modicum of glory and self-respect. A short lob was set up perfectly. Ken could see himself blasting the ball into the next province. For some unknown reason, Whitney did something totally out of character. As Ken was about to disintegrate the ball, Whitney flew out of nowhere, tackled Ken, and dropped the ball over the net just out of reach of their rampaging opponents.

Whitney laughed so hard he spilled his coffee. Ken sipped his coffee with a slight smile on his face. Underhill sort of giggled. The Israeli woman said good-bye; she had to leave for a class.

I was about to mention the final score when Ken pulled a piece of paper from his pocket and said, "Did I ever tell you my Harry Hopman story?"

I said, "No."

According to Ken, Harry Hopman had John Newcomb, Tony Roche, and Roy Emerson in a training session. Hopman had the three of them running through a variety of tortuous drills. Finally, after hours of running, hopping, and stopping on a dime, he had all three panting and begging for the showers. Hopman lined up all three men in the middle of the court, and told them that there was an American playing on Court 5, and under no circumstances where they to watch this American play for even a minute.

Obviously, Hopman was not familiar with the famous child therapist Dr. Spock. If he had, he would have never even mentioned Whitney Reed, because as soon as Hopman was out of sight the three men made a beeline for Court 5.

The next day, during a practice session featuring half-volleys, all three men twirled the racquet over their heads and took wild swings at the ball.

Harry Hopman stopped practiced and announced to everyone within a mile radius that somebody did something that they were told not to do.

Whitney spit his coffee all over the table. Underhill laughed so hard he almost slipped out of his chair. I couldn't breath for a moment, and was saved from passing out by Underhill slapping me on the back.

When Vance Packard announced to the world that it was the medium, not the message, he had to have known Ken

Sheffield. The Hopman story was very clever, but Ken's narration made it hysterical.

We all applauded for Ken to tell another story, and, why not, he was on a roll. Actually, Whitney applauded the loudest and the longest; he was on the edge of his seat, he was so excited he looked as though he was about to pee in his pants.

Ken sat back in his chair, sipped his coffee, and proceeded to entertain us with a litany of clever anecdotes:

François Godbout was a good player, probably the best in Canada at the time. He eventually lost to Whitney in the finals, but before he played Whitney, he had to get by Tom Brown.

Ken, Whitney, Godbout and several other players were in the player's lounge playing poker. Godbout looked at his watch and said he needed to get going, he had a match to play. Whitney looked up and asked whom he was playing. Godbout responded, Tom Brown.

Whitney said, "You'll be back soon."

Godbout mumbled something inaudible, like so's your old man, or your mother wears combat boots. Casually, Whitney referred to the fact that Brown hadn't lost a game and he was in the quarterfinals, and they might as well put the game on hold for a few minutes while Brown bashed Godbout off the court.

Godbout was back at the table in what seemed like 20 minutes. He sat down and said he didn't know what all the fuss was about Tom Brown – Godbout won in straight sets 6-2, 6-3.

Whitney, Underhill, and I looked at Ken waiting for something witty and clever to pop out of the Sheffield mouth.

Ken threw up his hands and said, "Give me a break; I'm just trying to show how unpredictable big-time tennis can be."

Ken leaned forward and said, "Whitney loved to play players who thought that they were really big hitters. He loved to play those big Type A personalities. The ones who think they can sleep with whomever they want, buy whatever they want, and generally feel that the world owes them a great big debt."

It was Mill Valley in the middle 1970s, Whitney was seeded No. 2 and his quarterfinal match was against one of the quintessentially big hitters around. The guy comes out swinging from the floor. In the first game, the guy serves and volleys the ball out. Instead of letting the ball bounce, Whitney returns the ball from the doubles alley. The guy winds up and lets fly with a huge forehand that was also out, but instead of letting the ball bounce, Whitney returns the ball to the middle of the court. The guy lets go of an inside out forehand that was again out, but Whitney refuses to take the point, and he returns the ball to the center of the court. Finally, the guy was so frustrated that he catches the ball and says, "I won the point."

Whitney laughed.

The referee said, point Reed.

The big hitter looked as though he was about too explode. He lost the first game and never recovered. Whitney went on to win easily.

I looked over at Whitney and asked if that story was true. Whitney said he took a chance. The big hitter had a reputation of coming out strong and blowing people off the court. Whitney went on to say that sometimes you get lucky when you throw a changeup.

We all looked at Ken. Ken sat back again and pulled the folded piece of paper from his pocket.

"Do any of you know the weirdest score ever recorded for a win?" asked Ken.

Everyone shook his head.

Ken proceeded to tell us about the weirdest score ever – 0-6, 0-5, 40-love, retired. Whitney was playing Conway Catton in Portola Valley. Dr. Catton was fast, and when he was on he could be tough to beat, but he was not in Whitney's class. Obviously, something was the matter with Whitney – too much of something the previous night.

Whitney was going through the motions figuring he'd be back in Alameda for an evening of gin rummy, maybe a little girl chasing, and, most assuredly, a beer or two. Connie hit a lob that Whitney ran for, flipped the ball over his shoulder, and, as luck would have it, the ball barely cleared the net. Catton ran like the wind, stopped, twisted awkwardly, and broke his leg.

Strangest score ever recorded, according to Ken Sheffield – 0-6, 0-5, 40-love, retired.

"How about something not related too tennis," I asked.

Underhill thought for a moment and said to Sheffield, "How about the Weillahan and Fitzgerald fracas."

"Yeah, good one," said Ken.

Consistent with Ken's wonderful narrations, he explained that Fitzgerald and Weillahan were varsity basketball players. Both were first-string and both had great jump shots.

Whitney could jump and he obviously had great hand-eye coordination, but he was no basketball player. Underhill and Sheffield were basketball players.

As Sheffield described the scene, Whitney started to squirm in his seat. It seems that Underhill, Sheffield, Whitney, and a bunch of guys were in the San Jose State gym shooting baskets. Someone said, let's choose sides, and play a game to 24. Underhill, Sheffield, and Whitney were on one side, and Weillahan, Fitzgerald, and another guy were on the other.

Sheffield articulates the fact that their time on the court will be very short.

Underhill nods in agreement.

Whitney says to Weillahan, "You guys ever gamble?"

Weillahan and Fitzgerald are all over gambling like a cheap suit.

Underhill and Sheffield feel like they'd rather be in Philadelphia.

Whether it was peer pressure, testosterone, or just plain foolishness, all six player took the court. Amazingly, both teams trade baskets to 22-all. Whitney would move to the center of the key, and Sheffield and Underhill would cut right and left for lay-ups or short jump shots. Weillahan and Fitzgerald would race around the court looking slightly amused hitting 18-foot jump shots at will.

At 22-all, Underhill passed to Sheffield, Sheffield lobbed the ball to Whitney. Both Underhill and Sheffield cut. Whitney faked to both players and went into his best Bevo Francis impression. Mind you, Whitney hasn't taken a shot in 22 points. Sheffield and Underhill danced around trying to attract Whitney's attention. Finally, Sheffield saw a huge gleam in

Whitney's eye – the same gleam that appeared in the NCAA final just before he blew an easy lead against Larry Nagler. Whitney grasped the ball in both hands, and from the free-throw line, lobbed the ball over his head into the basket.

Weillahan and Fitzgerald paid Ken, Dick, and Whitney, but first Weillahan made them promise that this little interlude never happened. He didn't say he would beat the shit out of them if word got out, but the implication was clear.

Dick and Ken were not surprised that Whitney flipped the ball over his head, nor were they surprised that it went in. They'd been around long enough to know that nothing about Whitney was a surprise.

Ken stood up and announced that he was late. He needed to pick up his 10-year-old son. Whitney jumped up and hugged Ken. We all shook hands and promised to do it again soon.

Underhill, Whitney and I headed downtown for a late lunch at the Washington Street Bar and Grill. After lunch, I drove Whitney home, and Underhill went off to work. Thirty years ago, we would have closed every bar in the City, and probably wound up in Reno spending all our remaining money in some sleazy cathouse. How times have changed.

More 1958 - 1959
Not Everybody Loves a Lover – Bob Hill

When Bob Hill roomed with Whitney at San Jose State, he ate nothing but yogurt. He ate nothing but yogurt because Whitney hated yogurt. Yogurt in those days was not the nice flavored variety of today. In 1960, yogurt was the next best thing to paste. It looked, tasted, and smelled like the stuff kindergarten kids used to eat and throw at one another.

Bob Hill bought yogurt because if he bought steak, Whitney would eat the steak before it had a chance to get cold in the refrigerator. Poor Bob would spend $25 on food, and, maybe he'd get to eat about $5 worth. Whitney would bring a bunch of fruit salad from home as his offering for the week's food supply, and Bob hated fruit salad

As you can imagine, Whitney was a horrible roommate. If he wasn't eating all the food in the house, he was setting fire to the couch with an errant cigarette, or creating an atmosphere of a smoky barroom with the ubiquitous open beer cans. Bob was not as forgiving as most of Whitney's buddies from that era, and when school started in 1961, Whitney needed to find another roommate.

Bob played doubles with Whitney in college from 1958 to 1960, and they did well. They won most of their matches because they simply outclassed most of the teams in the country. They'd lose a set now and then, mostly because of Whitney's quirkiness. At Stanford in 1959, they won the first set against Stanford's No. 1e team (Ogden/Nelson) 6-0. In the second set, Whitney felt that Bob made a bad call, so he tanked the second set. Bob and Whitney won the third set 6-0.

Alex Olmedo and Ed Atkinson notwithstanding, Bob and Whitney should have won the NCAA tournament in both 1959 and 1960. They lost in the quarterfinals both years. In 1959, it was too much booze, and in 1960 it was not enough food. In 1959, Whitney and his girlfriend spent the evening before the quarterfinals attempting to drink all the booze in the greater Chicago area, and in 1960, Whitney simply forgot to eat. When his blood sugar level went to 0%, Whitney's effort on the court went to 0%.

By 1960, Bob may have had his fill of babysitting Whitney. He had rescued him from every den of iniquity in the San Jose area, and for his effort, he had to eat yogurt for two years. He hauled Whitney to the hospital after Whitney got smashed in the eye playing a pickup basketball game, and he had to put gas in his car to get there. He was tired of living in a barroom environment. He knew Whitney's act intimately, and, as far as Bob was concerned, it was getting near the final curtain.

The NCAA singles final in 1959 was a contributing factor to the demise of the Hill/Reed relationship. Whitney was to play Donald Dell in the finals at noon, only Whitney was sacked out with his girlfriend at noon.

Bob tells this story with a serious lack of wonder and amazement. It seems the responsibility of getting Whitney to the courts on time fell on Bob. Butch Kirkorian, San Jose's tennis coach, was unavailable due to prior commitments, and that left Bob in the all-too-familiar role of babysitter.

Bob found Whitney in his hotel room all wrapped up in sheets, blankets, and his girlfriend. The room smelled like the amalgamation of a San Francisco Sixth and Mission bar, and a South Central LA gymnasium.

Bob shook Whitney and said, "Whitney, the finals were at noon and it's twelve thirty."

Whitney looked up and said, "Who won?"

Whitney was incredibly lucky Marty Riessen's dad was running the tournament, and, for whatever reason, Riessen's dad let Whitney play the final.

Whitney won easily in straight sets.

In 1964, Bob and Whitney reconciled. They played together for three more years. According to Bob, 1964, 1965, 1966 were not unlike their college years. They'd win some big matches if Whitney was prepared to play, and they'd lose if he wasn't.

Bob obviously has more guts and integrity then most of us. Most of us would have been satisfied to play with Whitney in any condition. Bob did not, and he decided that all the worry was not worth the advantages. Winning a national title one day and having your ulcer operated on the next was no way to live.

In 1966, Bob had had enough. It was time to "slipped out the back, Jack." He couldn't take the inconsistency, never knowing which Whitney Reed would show up for a tournament. He eventually teamed up with Erick Van Dillen and they did very well together. They had several great wins, probably the biggest was over Torbin Ulrich and Jan Leschly.

Today Bob and his wife live in Palm Desert. He looks great, paints a few houses, and plays a lot of tennis. When he considers the time he spent on the court with Whitney, I don't sense a great deal of acrimony. He simply tried to make an uncomfortable situation workable. Bob knew Whitney was just playing Whitney and, unlike God, Bob was not amused.

- CHAPTER 7 -

Next Stop,
Tour Life

Tennis players, the world-class variety, did not earn a bundle of money practicing their craft. Unlike today's players, they didn't have coaches, trainers, and publicists. They had patrons of sorts, and every once in a while a player would fall into a situation that was too good to believe. Whitney flew in a military aircraft from Palm Springs to San Juan, Puerto Rico for a tournament. The story is a little sketchy, but Whitney had just won the Palm Springs Invitational, he was sitting at the bar in the Racquet Club having a few beers with a Charlie Farrell when he realized that he missed his connection out of Palm Springs International Airport. Farrell said no problem. He made a phone call and the next thing Whitney knew, he was in an aircraft with distinct Air Force markings heading for San Juan.

Charlie Farrell must have thought that a trip to San Juan sounded good, because he brought along Vera Ellen for company. Charlie called Whitney Chauncie. He'd holler across the tennis court. "Whitney, it's tea time." On the trip to San Juan "tea time" lasted from takeoff until they returned to Palm Springs. Vic Seixas won the tournament mainly because he was lucky enough to miss most of "tea time." Situations like Whitney's lucky trip to San Juan happened, but, for the most part, tour players of Whitney's era were like Gypsies, traveling from one tournament to another without the guarantee of appearance money or a place to sleep.

Before the ATP and open tennis, being a tour player was tough all the way around. The competition was horrendous. Players traveled all over the world playing tennis for silver cups, hot dogs, and half a loaf of bread. Whitney was literally on the streets hitching a ride from one tournament to another. If a player received an airline ticket from a tournament promoter, he immediately sought the carrier to relinquish the ticket and finagled a cheaper way to travel. Jack Frost made a science out of travel manipulation. (More on Jack Frost later)

Tour Life in Berkeley?

The Berkeley Tennis Club has hosted the Pacific Coast Tennis Championships every year since about 100 years before the free speech movement. The Club is the coolest tennis club west of Newport, and about three miles from Whitney's front door. Obviously, lodging was not an issue, but transportation was an issue. He could ride with his dad, he could borrow his dad's car, or he could bum a ride from one of the competitors. As we will soon discover, bumming a ride from a fellow competitor was not a very good idea.

The 1960 edition of the Pacific Coast Tennis Championships featured a gaggle of great players: Barry MacKay, Marty Riessen, Dennis Ralston, and Whitney. In the quarterfinals, Whitney lost a close match to Riessen and was eliminated. MacKay beat Ralston and wound up in the finals against Riessen. In 1960 all the drama was not confined between the white lines of the tennis courts at the Berkeley Tennis Club. In fact, the extracurricular activities off the court made the 1960 Pacific Coast Tennis Championships' on-court activities seem amazingly dull.

There was always a party, because parties were an integral part of tour life. Whitney loved the social part of being a tour player, and he hated to miss a party as much as he hated to lose a tennis match. At any tournament from Wimbledon to Forest Hills, the first question he posed to the tour director after he checked the seedings was, "Where's the party?"

The post-quarterfinal party during the 1960 Pacific Coast Championships was held in Orinda, California. As the crow flies, Orinda is not very far from the Berkeley Tennis Club, about a mile and a half. Traversing the Berkeley Hills is the issue; unless you want to drive to Chico, you need to negotiate the Caldecott Tunnel.

Whitney thought it a bit embarrassing to ask your dad to drive you to a party. A 28-year-old guy being dropped off at party by his father may be viewed in some circles as odd. Whitney asked Barry MacKay instead. MacKay had borrowed a car from Jim Mc Manus' brother for the duration of the tournament. MacKay knew Whitney was always good fun, and when he got into the swing of a party, he was great fun. Barry complied, knowing Whitney tagging along meant that the party would be anything but dull.

Barry, Betty Hannis, Whitney's current squeeze, and Whitney headed off to the party in Orinda. The drive through the Caldecott Tunnel was negotiated without incident.

Orinda is not Palm Beach, Orinda is a sleepy little town where the big event is when the Orinda movie theater features an R-rated movie. Everything considered, Whitney was enjoying himself. He had a couple of glasses of champagne, and managed to deflect the advances of two very interested female admirers, a blonde-haired cutie from Cardiff-by-the-Sea and a socialite from San Francisco. Both interludes left a glaring Betty Hannis tapping her foot in unbridled annoyance. By early evening, Whitney had enough of the party, and was definitely ready to move on. Barry and Betty voiced a similar desire, so the trio decided to call it an evening.

All went well on the drive home until they reached the tunnel. Barry enjoyed driving fast, and Whitney has always been something of an Adrenalin junkie – a potentially lethal combination. They roared through the mouth of the tunnel, and into the bowels of the tunnel proper. Actually, racing into the tunnel is nothing every resident of Contra Costa County under 30 has not done a million times. A problem occurs when all three people in the front seat decide to change the radio station simultaneously. A disaster occurs when the non-driving duo looks up and sees two red brake lights glaring astonishingly close.

Barry MacKay has very good reflexes; if he didn't, Whitney, Barry, and Betty would be residing in very cramped quarters in a Colma cemetery. No actually, only Barry and the Betty would be in Colma. Whitney, as a veteran, would be in the vet cemetery at the Presidio in San Francisco. Fortunately for everyone, Barry's reflexes prevailed, he slammed on the brakes, and steered the car literally up the side of the tunnel. The car rolled over on its top, and resembled the launching of a Vandenberg missile as it shot out the west end of the tunnel. Miraculous driving or unbelievable luck, the car slid to a stop without making contact with anything stouter than shrub eucalyptus saplings and a variety of wild grasses.

Luckily for Barry, Whitney, and Betty, the Oakland Fire Department was in the process of cleaning up a previous accident. A grizzled old firefighter peeked into the up-side-down car and asked if anyone was hurt. It was the perfect opportunity to make a comment for the ages, but Whitney, Barry, and the Betty were all wrapped up in each other: arms, legs, heads, and torsos connected, and in their proper places.

When the smoke had cleared, Whitney called his dad who promptly raced to the crash scene, restored order, and then drove everyone to his and her respective places. Barry won the tournament, unaffected by the drama of the previous day.

Whitney gave the next tournament a brief consideration, and then headed for the coolest bar in Oakland (The Kings X) to play some gin rummy.

Poor Betty Hannis. Whitney went on to play Davis Cup, and Betty went on to nurse a broken heart.

- CHAPTER 8 -

Some Random Thoughts and Shoddy Shots

In Whitney Reed's time, most of the elite players in the world were quasi- professionals, meaning professionals in attitude and lifestyle, without cell phones, iPods, and Blackberries. They lived better than most rock stars – when they finally made it to a tournament. They traveled more than any jet setter on the planet – most of the time in beat-up jalopies. Their list of acquaintances was spotted with the rich and famous – even the rich and famous love to be near elite athletes. The only dissimilarities between the players of today and the players of Whitney's time was the size of their bank accounts and the size of their entourage.

Most of Whitney's contemporaries dreaded the day when the ride would end, but not Whitney, because for Whitney the ride would never end. Only the grim reaper would keep Whitney off of a tennis court

Whitney can't remember when he was not playing on a tennis court, or leaving to go play on a tennis court, or just coming off of a tennis court. His life was a collage of green and red concrete, various shades of red to beige clay, and dark green closely cropped grass. In between one tournament or another, there were a few card games, a few beers, and a few women to pass the time. For a little beer money, he would pursue an occasional gig as a paperboy, taxi driver, and car attendant. These interludes, from card games to taxi driving, had a finite quality, never lasting more than a few months, because nothing even remotely compared with tennis as source of fulfillment. If you ask him how he survived all those years, he would mumble, clear his throat a few times, and acknowledge that he hadn't a clue.

Contemporary thought dictates that professional tennis players aren't supposed to play cards all night, professional tennis players aren't supposed to have hangovers, and professional tennis players aren't supposed to considered beer, bourbon, and a pack of Marlboros as integral parts of pre-match preparations. Whitney Reed considered all the above as life's essentials. Whitney could party all night and compete with the best tennis players in the world all day. His closest friends maintained that he was at his best when he was playing in that gray area between inebriation and an excellent hangover. What only a few friends understood was that Whitney needed downtime to play his finest tennis. He was such a fierce competitor that without the opportunity to deflate, he was not his best. A standing bit of levity that later became an urban legend was after winning the State Fair tournament in Sacramento in 1962, he discovered the results of the match when he called a friend to ask about a trophy he found in the front seat of his car – Jim Nelson says it's true and Whitney won't comment.

Whitney was, in his playing days, much more then the beer-guzzling, cigarette-smoking comic of the USLTA. He was an individualist, a gentleman, and a frightful competitor. Whitney believed that tournament tennis was no different than an actor's part in a play or a musician's solo in a concerto. As a participant, he was a thespian in pursuit of the perfect performance, and anyone watching deserved the very best presentation he could offer. Allen Fox called him bizarre and Bud Collins called him zany, but they both agree that Whitney is a unique personality on and off the court.

Maybe no one knows Whitney intimately, and maybe that's good. He is fun, sad, and enigmatic. An elusive character with an almost cult following. Kindred spirits celebrate his successes and empathize with his failures. Just the mention of his name in some circles is good for hours of reminiscing.

Yet, in every discussions involving Whitney, one aphorism persists. Whitney was always Whitney. He was the same person accepting a trophy or heading for the locker room. As Jackie Cooper, former junior Davis Cupper, director of tennis at the Jackie Cooper Tennis Center in Palm Desert, and all-around cool guy, remarked recently, "Whitney was the same guy winning at Forest Hills or losing in Hoboken."

Being a friend of Whitney's came with huge risks. Primarily, anyone foolish enough to emulate Whitney's midnight meanderings was either dumb or suicidal. The Australians enjoyed big reputations as fun-loving, skirt-chasing beer drinkers, but they were mere amateurs compared to Whitney. If Newcomb, Emerson, or Roche had lived as fast as Whitney, their names would not appear in the record books. They would appear on head stones. Instead of enjoying a prominent place in Bud Collins' History of Tennis, they'd have a small spot in the Boston Globe's obituary column. Occasionally a player would join the tour and see Whitney's classic third set recovery and think: Hell, if Whitney can do it so can I. Presently, they're either dead or teaching tennis in Peoria.

- CHAPTER 9 -

More Shoddy Thoughts

At the 1960 Cincinnati stop, Whitney met Ed Atkinson, a first- year tour player and the proud possessor of the biggest forehand on the tour. If tour players at the time had required guardians or coaches, Whitney and Ed would have been summarily separated. No self-respecting coach would have allowed two athletes to feed on each other's penchant for life's more festive activities. Fortunately, they were both endowed with ox-like constitutions and they survived without causing each other permanent damage. In fact, Whitney taught Ed to concentrate on the middle ball if three balls appeared to be coming across the net.

To be completely fair, the '50s and the '60s embraced a different set of standards. Executives thought nothing of a three-martini lunch with a pack of cigarettes and a couple highballs after work. They ate fatty red meat, they devoured pasta with tons of cheese and cream, and if they made it to 65 they were lucky. A man was judged by how well he handled liquor, tobacco, and fashion. It was cool to drink copious amounts of booze; it was uncool to drink copious amounts of booze and act like a bore. It was cool to smoke; it was uncool to dress like a slob. Whitney Reed was always quintessentially cool. In 60 years of competitive tennis, no one has ever accused Whitney of being a bore or a slob.

Understanding Whitney's proclivity for the good life is a major dilemma for some people, but not for Jack Frost, John Newcomb, or any other tennis player of that era. They figured out at a very young age that tennis was his or her ticket to ride. They understood that they could have almost everything enjoyable in life and not have to sell one shoe, drive one nail, or don one three-piece suit. They could enjoy the company of interesting people, and appreciate the companionship of beautiful women. All they needed to do was hit a little ball over a three-foot net. Tennis allowed them to spend the spring in New England, the fall in the Caribbean, and the summer in Europe. Whitney and most of his contemporaries understood that the life they choose was finite. Time would take its toll. The design of the human body was at odds with the physical abuse that is inherent in the game – not to mention the abuse generated by the lifestyle. Where Whitney's attitudes and goals differed from his colleagues was in his core value. He was a performer first. Winning was important, ranking was important, and ego was important. However, in front of either one or a million fans, if he could stroll into "no man's land" and half-volley an opponent's passing shot for a winner, he was in pure heaven.

Whitney's story is not without precedence; countless storied athletes lived life in the fast lane. Mickey Mantle died in his 60s. Bobby Lane never made 60. John Brodie had a stroke and barely survived. What separated Whitney and made him unique was that John Brodie, Mickey Mantle, Bobby Lane, and countless other professional athletes were forced to quit their beloved sport by sheer attrition. They got old. Except for Brodie, who played on the senior golf tour, 99 percent of the retired athletes either became sports announcers or played golf full time. When interviewed, they universally proclaimed that the competition is the element they missed the most. Not Whitney, he never gave a hoot about the competition, he only cared about the performance. On the Caribbean tour, he beat Emerson and Fraser in the same day to win a tournament. Ironically, if there was no one in the stands to enjoy his feat he would have considered the day no different than sitting at his kitchen table working the New York Times crossword puzzle and completing it successfully.

- CHAPTER 10 -

Anything Worth Doing
Is Worth Doing to Excess

Each year during the Southampton (Meadow Club) stop on the tour, a very nice family opened their home for the tour players. The home naturally became the headquarters for all the social activity during tour week. Ed Atkinson remarked that if you were looking for anything or anyone connected to the tournament all you needed to do was show up any morning and search for a familiar face. The effort usually involved turning over bodies in various stages of recovery. Prudently, the family usually vacationed in Europe during the tournament and returned when their neighbors, the house cleaning service, and the local constabulary declared it safe.

The 1963 Southampton tournament was noteworthy because it was a paradigm of Whitney's life on tour. The basic story line would replay itself countless times until he sashayed into no man's land and half-volleyed a drop shot winner for the last time.

The setting was the semifinals of the 1963 Southampton Championships. The match was just hours away. Whitney slipped through the quarterfinals and celebrated with a cute little blonde from Manhattan Beach. Celebrated may be an understatement; the last thing Whitney remembered was the little blonde trying to convince him to play mixed doubles in her father's tennis club championships wearing a disguise. Now, he had to drag himself out of bed and play Kozei Kamo, who drank nothing more than a glass of warm milk with dinner and was in bed by 9 p.m.

Whitney looked in the mirror and decided shaving was way too dangerous. Good thing tennis players have tanned faces, he thought; hides the effects of over-celebrating. Besides, baseball pitchers never shave on the day of a game. Maybe a little stubble would bring him some luck – he'd need it, because he was certain that Kamo didn't feel this bad.

He wondered how much fun he had had the previous night, vaguely remembering the blonde, a bottle of Jim Beam, other assorted playmates, and a drive to the beach with Atkinson. No matter, he always played better with a touch of last night and a slight hangover. He climbed into a pair of white shorts and pulled on a white shirt, reached for his beat-up Jack Kramer racquet, and headed for the Club.

According to Atkinson, Whitney made it to the courts safely and on time. According to the record Whitney won in five sets. As Ed's story goes, Whitney lost the first two sets, won the third set 7-5 and during the break between the third and fourth sets ran to the bar and ordered five beers. He placed them strategically between his tennis bag and the water cooler. During every crossover he sipped from one of the cups until at the end of the match all the cups were empty. Also empty was Kozei Kamo; Whitney hit lob after lob followed by drop shot after drop shot until Kamo was totally spent. Kamo must have run 400 miles in that two-hour match.

When Whitney returned to the beach house, Ed was on the couch with a cold pack on his forehead.

He opened one terribly red eye and asked, "How did you do?"

Whitney replied, "6-0 in the fifth."

Ed said, "I am in the presence of greatness."

Can't Leave Ed Without Remembering his Wedding in 1978

Ed Atkinson's wedding in 1978 was a rocking affair. It was staged at the Los Angeles Tennis Club, and everyone who was anyone participated.

Whitney played an integral part in the affair by setting a new world record for champagne consumption. It was an extraordinary feat because there were some extraordinary drinkers at that wedding -- extraordinary drinkers and extraordinarily beautiful women. In fact, the whole reception area had the distinct feeling of movie set. At any moment you'd expect to see Cary Grant sharing a drink with Ingrid Bergman.

Whitney was between wives and girl friends at the time, and it took a New York minute to fall in love. There was a plethora of available, attractive women, but who caught his eye was the cutest blonde imaginable. She couldn't care less about tennis or tennis players; she was looking for a studio contract. Consequently, she had no idea who the sleepy-eyed, gravelly-voiced person was who kept pouring champagne into her glass. As Whitney remembered, the initial dialogue with the blonde was pretty inane; she kept asking why everyone had such a great tan.

The blonde was cool, the reception terrific, but Whitney needed to be in Australia to play in a Grand Masters tournament, and he only had a few hours to get to the airport. The plane left LAX at 4:30 p.m., and it was already 2:30. Anyone who knew Whitney was aware that getting to an airport on time was about 25th on Whitney list of important matters, just before eating spinach and just after court dates.

Whitney and the blonde where leaning against the bar, looking deep into each others eyes, sipping champagne, and planning a night snuggled in silk sheets. The blonde had the look of: Well, I think I'll worry about my acting career tomorrow when someone (Who remains anonymous, but has the initials EA) whispered in her perfectly shaped ear that the sleepy-eyed gentleman next to her was a famous athlete who needed to be on an airplane. Further, if he missed the flight, the fate of the free world was in the balance.

Fortunately, the blonde didn't question the relationship between athletics and the free world. She simply shook off the miasma emanating from an expensive champagne, and her charming companion, and literally jumped into action mode. She called for a limo; took a full glass of champagne from Whitney and replaced it with coffee; found Ed and made Whitney recite a litany of appropriate remarks concerning life, love, and happiness. Finally, she grabbed Whitney by the hand and steered him in the direction of the waiting limo. On the steps of the LA Tennis Club she hugged and kissed Whitney, slipped her phone number in his pocket, and warned the limo driver that he would suffer an indescribable fate if Whitney missed the plane.

Years later, Whitney mused, "I should have married that girl."

Whitney opened his eyes 24 hours later as the plane was making its final approach to Brisbane airport. Actually, it may not have been the first time he opened his eyes; he vaguely remembered a flight attendant suggesting that he could be more comfortable in the rear of the plane. The flight was half empty and whole rows were open. He could stretch out and sleep unbothered by the rest of the passengers. The only time he had to move was to go to the bathroom, eat a meal, and smile at the attractive flight attendants.

Malcolm Anderson was the tournament director. He enticed Whitney to make the trip with visions of dancing girls and poker games; actually, Whitney would have made the trip without the enticements. Australians were cool people, always ready for a game of chance and another round of beers. Too bad they were such good tennis players; it would have been fun not hating them.

As Whitney waited in line for his baggage, he was beginning to feel pretty good. He had about 20 hours sleep, some good food, and plenty of attention. All things considered, except for missing the blonde, he was pleased he had made the trip.

He watched the luggage go around and around the carousel. During the fifth trip by his station, he was beginning to get a little anxious. By the tenth trip he was in full panic mode. Finally, the full realization, his clothes, racquets, and shoes did not make the trip from L.A. He was in Brisbane, Australia, and all he had was the clothes on his back.

Crisis is not the state of mind that affects everyone with equal consideration. Crisis mode for Whitney is like an evening at the symphony for a NASCAR enthusiast. An uncomfortable situation but nothing an extra martini can't handle.

Whitney's Brisbane crisis was annoying because playing tennis in loafers and a Hawaiian shirt was not going to please Malcolm Anderson. The first problem, from Whitney's perspective, was a racquet. He knew Hugh Stewart was always prepared. Hugh was a very good at getting the most out of everything. Free equipment, appearance money, and the best accommodation, if it was possible to get, Hugh would get it. The nice thing about Hugh was that he was always willing to share.

So Whitney called Hugh's hotel and solved dilemma No. 1 - - a racquet. Sub-dilemma No. 1 was Hugh played with a huge racquet, extra heavy and extra long. Whitney said, "It took a friggin' wheelbarrow to lug the thing on to the court."

The subsequent annoying issues -- shoes, shirts, and shorts -- were dealt with in a very surreptitious manner. He borrowed one piece of clothing from ten different sources. Actually, it was pretty creative. He just walked up to Frank Sedgeman and said, "Hey Frank, can I borrow a pair of socks." When you consider that there were 64 players in the draw, Whitney could have borrowed enough outfits to last the rest of the season.

So when he showed up to play Torben Ulrich in the first round he was christened the fashion Frankenstein: Sedgeman socks, Emerson shoes, and Olmedo shorts.

Torben Ulrich was almost Whitney's equal in zaniness. He was tall, left-handed, and had great legs. That was not Whitney's observation; it was the consensus of opinion from a variety of women who followed Torben's matches with great interest.

Whitney roomed with Torben on many occasions, all of them eventful. For Whitney, rooming with Torben was almost as much fun as performing. He never knew who would come knocking at their bedroom door. What he did know was Torben's favorite method of answering the door. Torben would make sure the knocker was one or more female admirers, then he'd take all his clothes off and rip the door open. Some times it worked and sometimes it didn't. Torben said the fresh air on a naked body was good for the soul. Whitney said Torben was just horny.

According to the ATP computer, Torben played Whitney only once, and that was in Sacramento. Whitney won easily in straight sets. What the ATP computer didn't show was the results from Brisbane.

Whitney first knew he was in trouble when he had to ask a ball boy to help him get Hugh's racquet out of his bag. Then his borrowed clothes didn't fit well, and the night before the match nobody showed up at Torben's door, resulting in an early bedtime.

Whitney lost the first set so fast it was like he walked onto the court, warmed up, and the referee said, "First set to Mr. Ulrich." The number of point he won where so few that the referee could keep score in his head. Whitney managed to keep it close in the second set but by five-all his arm was so sore he was sure he had suffered terminal tennis elbow. Torben went on to win the match, much to the pure pleasure of the bevy of female fans in the stands, many of whom saw a considerable amount of Torben's anatomy the night before.

Most athletes would feel a touch of remorse if they had traveled 5,000 miles to play in a tennis tournament with no racquet, no clothes, and no chance of success. Not Whitney, his purpose has always been clearly defined: play competitively, have fun, and be entertaining in the process. From Whitney's perspective, his trip Down Under was resounding success. He had fun, and his match with Torben was very entertaining, especially to the women in the audience. He didn't play competitively, but so what, succeeding in two out of three goals isn't too bad. If he played baseball he would be batting .667.

So when he boarded United Flight 344, nonstop to San Francisco, he had no regrets other than a small nagging sensation that Malcolm may be a bit annoyed. He should have beaten Torben easily, and he should have won the tournament. He just got caught up in the moment, having all that fun playing in front of Torben's fan club. How could he have disappointed all those beautiful women; it would be un-Whitney, un-American.

- CHAPTER 11 -

Where's
Merion Pennsylvania

The Merion Cricket Club, on the Main Line outside Philadelphia, was part of the Eastern Tennis Circuit in those days. In its 1960 incarnation Whitney slipped through the first few rounds without much effort – a feat in itself. In those years there were 64 players on the tour, 64 of the best players in the world. Every match was a test. A player could draw Rod Laver the first morning of the tournament and be off to the next tour stop by noon. Conversely, a second tiered player could get hot and beat a couple of guys and wind up in the finals. And it happened more than once. Allen Fox, a college player from UCLA, had a run where he beat Ashley Cooper, Neal Frazier, and Roy Emerson on consecutive days.

Whitney played Tony Vincent in the quarterfinals and won. An observer at courtside said Whitney appeared to be slightly amused by the whole match. Jack Frost, a tour player and fellow adventurer the previous night, maintained that Whitney was still "in his cups" for most of the match.

Whitney ambled around the court, mainly at the service line hitting vintage drop shots and crosscourt lobs that had an uncanny knack of finding those four square inches where the back line and sideline meet. Vincent would hit his forehand as hard as he could (Vincent was no Laver in the power department) and Whitney would seemingly catch the ball lightly on his racquet, and magically the ball would drop like a wounded duck just out of Tony's reach. When Whitney was "in the zone," an Arthur Ashe phrase, he was virtually impossible to beat. And he was in the zone that day. Sometime around the third set, Vincent became frustrated, so frustrated that people on the sideline though he was going to burst. His face became bright red; his respiration hit the danger zone, and there were little bits of spittle all over the court. Whitney seemed to get stronger as Tony grew weaker. When the match finally ended Vincent threw down his racquet, looked at Whitney, and shook his head.

Later in the locker room, Whitney needed to haul a chair into the shower, because standing was too difficult. As the hot water beat down on Whitney's body, still dressed in tennis clothes, Allison Danzig, tennis editor for the New York Times, asked if there were any more guys like him in Northern California. Whitney replied, "Not any more, they're all dead."

- CHAPTER 12 -

A Return
To Paradise

When Whitney returned from the service in 1957 there was no doubt in his mind that he was destined to return to competitive tennis. He was a tennis player and that was that. His family would have preferred that he entertain the idea of gainful employment, but that was not in the cards. Whitney entered the Pacific Coast Championships at the Berkeley Tennis Club in 1957 as an unranked player. In fact, he had to qualify. In the first round, he played Jack Frost, a great player and presently a member of the Northern California Tennis Hall of Fame. Jack was ranked No. 9 in the country in 1961.

Whitney was relaxed, and not well rested. He had his ration of excitement the night before the match, consequently the Frost matchup was competitive, but it was Whitney s day, and he won in straight sets.

The second round match was against Art Larsen from San Leandro. Art had been ranked No. 3 in the United States behind Tony Trabert and Vic Seixas. Larsen was the heir-apparent to tennis royalty in the U.S., a fantastic player. He was, for a time, almost unbeatable. When he took the court against Whitney, the rumor was that an agreement had been reached between the two players. During the first set, Larsen would go easy on Whitney because of his Air Force tour and lack of tournament play; also, a good showing against Larsen would help Whitney's seeding for future tournaments. However, after the first set on all bets were supposed to be off.

This agreement was conjecture as far as Whitney was concerned. He had just spent four years in the service; he had nothing to lose. Whitney's recollection of the first set was slightly muddled. At 4-3 on the crossover he remembers Larsen whispering in his ear something about all bets being off.

Whitney broke Larsen's serve at 4-all, and then went on to win the first set 6-4. The second set was furiously fought. Larsen attacked the net and Whitney hit lobs and drop shots; then Whitney attacked the net and Larsen missed lobs and drop shots. Whitney's game against his boyhood idol was superb. He showed none of the rust that should have accumulated over the four-year hiatus from big time tennis. As Art became more tentative, Whitney became more assertive. When Art's shots started to miss and Whitney's returns started to hit, the effect was concisely destructive and crushing in its finality. Larsen walked off the court at the end of the second set and wrapped his racquet around the net pole. The score: 6-4 Reed.

According to Linda Vale Van Der Meer, former wife of the famous teaching pro Dennis Van Der Meer, Whitney was "in the zone" that afternoon. She recalls Whitney gliding around the court effortlessly, looking slightly satisfied, lobbing or dropping the ball just out of reach. Larsen had tried to unleash his patented touch game but every shot seemed a day late and a dollar short. Her description of the match ending was considerably more entertaining than Whitney's was. Linda said that Larsen, after crushing his racquet around the net poll, proceeded to rant and rave all the way down Ashby Avenue on his way home to San Leandro.

In the quarterfinal match, Whitney was pitted against Tut Bartzen. In the USLTA rankings, Tut was ranked No. 4 in 1955, No. 5 in 1956 and then No. 4 again in 1958, and inducted into the USPTA Hall of Fame in 2003. He was the tennis coach at TCU until his retirement in 1999. Bartzen had a great career in tennis and participated in some good wins along the way. However, the quarters at the Pacific Coast Championships were not one of them. Whitney won again in straight sets. Tut was never in the match. Once again, Whitney displayed none of the rust that should have accumulated over the previous four years. He ran down every ball, and, miraculously, every return touched a line. Tut was gracious in the defeat, and Whitney moved on to face Vic Seixas in the semifinals.

The semifinals were played in the morning with the fog and dew barely off the court. It was cold and damp. Whitney couldn't seem to get started or develop any rhythm. Seixas served and volleyed and maintained constant pressure. Maybe it was the rust finally showing through, but every lob and every drop shot fell a little too long or dropped a little too short. Not even a night on the town helped. (Whitney maintained that he only lost when there wasn't enough bar time to properly prepare for an important match.) Vic was older and on the downside of his illustrious career. Whitney should have won, but when you live by the touch, you can sometimes die by the touch.

- CHAPTER 13 -

The Best of Friends,
The Best of Times

Whitney met Dennis Hennessee at the South Shore Beach and Tennis club in Alameda. Dennis was the head football coach at Alameda High School and a fair tennis player. Whitney was the tennis pro, gin rummy player, and resident celebrity. It wasn't friends at first sight; it was sort of mutually ignoring one another. They'd walk by each other in the locker room, and go about the business that is prevalent in most country club locker rooms: setting up matches, scheduling lessons, showering, and going to the john. One afternoon at lunch, Dennis was talking to a couple of members about the big-time gin games that were played at the King's X in Oakland. Whitney overheard the conversation and, out of the blue, asked Dennis if he could join the next sojourn to downtown Oakland. Dennis said he was up for a little gin that evening and was leaving the club at 6 p.m. sharp. Whitney said something to the effect of "count me in." Whitney, without another word, got up and promptly left the dining room.

Dennis was still working for the school district in Alameda and had teaching responsibilities all afternoon. He didn't think much more about Whitney's comment. And with Whitney's gruff voice and laconic manner it was tough to tell when he was being serious or just being courteous. It wasn't in Dennis's mind that an actual date had been made, and it was only by sheer accident that he made the rendezvous at 6 p.m. He happened to stop by the club to pick up a gym bag. Whitney was standing in front of the club dressed in gin rummy playing clothes. Dennis, always thinking on his feet, opened the car door and said, "Let's get at it." They played gin all night, then Dennis, being employed, and Whitney, being the resident celebrity, drove off to their separate destinations: Dennis to Alameda High School and Whitney to bed. That was in 1971 and they have been friends ever since.

Dennis was a good influence on Whitney if one can say Billy Martin was a good influence on Mickey Mantle. Dennis traveled with Whitney to various tournaments and Whitney would introduce him as his manager and trainer. People who were friends and co-conspirators of the player and manager knew it was a new form of the blind leading the blind. Whitney did whatever Whitney wanted to do, and that was usually what Dennis wanted to do.

- Chapter 14 -

All That Glitters is Not Always a Sure Thing

The Grand Masters tour, an early tour for former champions and No. 1-rated players, was a great venue for Whitney. There was a little prize money, many parties, and a plethora of attractive women to enjoy.

In 1978, the Los Angeles Tennis Club hosted a stop on the Grand Masters Tour. The Los Angeles Tennis Club is a legendary place and home court to some of the best players of all times. Some of the more imaginative members maintain that the ghosts of Budge, Tilden, Vines, Riggs, and Gonzales still haunt center court.

Ed Atkinson picked up Whitney and Dennis at the airport and announced that the first stop was a party in Westwood. Dennis looked at Whitney and said, "What did we do to be so lucky?"

The home in Westwood was spectacular. It had a Gatsby-like appearance, a big circular drive framed by a plethora of rare trees and hedges – the ubiquitous Rolls Royce in the driveway. The front door was as large as the entry to the Hearst Castle, and seemed excessively big for the petite woman who welcomed them. She pointed to the bar and told them that there were bathing suits in the pool house. Dennis whispered to Whitney that swimming was for ducks and geese, and he was interested in the bar and dance floor. Whitney agreed and they made a beeline for the bar area. The bar was located in the middle of an area that looked like a combination gym and auditorium. Men and women roamed around in various stages of inebriation. Some were in swimwear; some were in sports wear. Everyone was deep in conversation, drinks in hand. Whitney and Dennis filtered though the party, dancing with whoever was available. As the night progressed, more and more of the partiers called it quits. Some were carried off; others managed on their own. It had to be late when Dennis and

Whitney realized that they were alone, in the middle of the dance floor, with two very attractive women. Dennis was the first to feel that not all was right with the world: they were having too much fun, and they knew nothing about the women in such close proximity.

As Dennis was agonizing over the beautiful woman firmly ensconced in his arms, he heard a sound that is everyone's worst nightmare: "What's going on here?" Dennis looked up and saw, making his way down the circular staircase, the biggest, scariest-looking man alive. (The circular staircase led directly into the auditorium, a.k.a., party room) The guy looked like the Rock without the cute arched eyebrow. Dennis reacted as if he was going for a drop volley. He grabbed Whitney by the arm and hurled him through the French doors leading to the pool area. They jumped the smallest of the shrubs adjacent to the driveway and ran all the way to downtown Westwood. They stopped, looked around, and figured the "Rock" was either slow, or the stark terror made them unusually fast. Just off Beverly Boulevard, they caught a cab, and made it to the hotel before sunrise.

Dennis was aware of Whitney's first-round match, but that was irrelevant. There was no way he could make Whitney abandon a party in full progress. He gave up that pursuit a long time ago. Had Whitney's opponent been the Pope, the evening would have proceeded as usual: "Wine, women, mirth, and laughter."

Whitney was playing Pancho Gonzalez in the first round, and quite possibly Pancho was having as much fun midnight marauding as Whitney and Dennis. Nobody knew for sure where Pancho did his carousing. Pancho played his social life very close to the vest. Whitney coaxed him into joining a few late-night sojourns, but not often. Whitney had a great affinity for Pancho, and he always wanted to play well either with him or against him. However, when Whitney walked onto the court for his first-round match, one glance at Pancho and Whitney knew his erstwhile friend was in a horrible mood. It was tough to play against Pancho when he was in a good mood; in a good mood, he only tried to beat you with a tennis racquet. The morning of the Grand Masters with Pancho in a foul mood, any player but Whitney would fear for his survival.

Whitney was returning serve extremely well. According to Whitney, when he returned well, the rest of his game went well. He roamed the center of the court in true Whitney fashion, hitting lobs off the volley and executing drop shots from the baseline. He won the first set 6-3.

In the second set Pancho and Whitney held serve until Whitney broke to go ahead 5-4. Dennis was in the upstairs bar figuring how he was going to protect Whitney's winnings. Maybe this was going to be one tournament where they made enough money to pay the bar-tab? Dennis was knee deep in euphoria with thoughts of solvency for Whitney. He didn't notice the object of the previous night's fantasy sweep into the bar on the arm of her husband.

Suddenly, the morning started to take a nosedive. Up pops the wife and the monster husband. Dennis's first thought was to make a run for it, but Mr. and Mrs. Monster were standing in the middle of the only way out. He frantically looked around for a place to hide. The restroom was out of the question, and he'd rather get the stuffing kicked out of him then dive behind the bar. Finally, Dennis decided that he was not going to go quietly into the night; he was going to duke it out with Mr. Monster. The problem was Mr. Monster was paying no attention to Dennis. In fact, no one was paying attention to Dennis. Everyone in the bar was watching Pancho having an apoplectic fit. The appearance of the wife and her monster husband was stressful enough, but the site of Pancho having a screaming fit on the court made the probability of a cardiac infarction a genuine possibility.

Pancho, at 5-4 Whitney, was challenging a call in the most vociferous manner. He was livid. Any other player alive short of Don Budge would have been disqualified. Whitney stood on the baseline stupefied. He was a couple of points from beating a tennis legend and his energy was draining as fast as a NASCAR racer's gas tank.

Pancho called for the referee, the tournament sponsors, and the mayor of Los Angeles. He was about to involve the President, when after 20 minutes peace somehow was restored. By this time Whitney's metabolism was at ground zero. No sleep, the chase through the bushes, and an interview with Wonder Woman had taken a final toll. Whitney dropped the last two sets 7-5 and 7-5.

Dennis was bewildered. The object of the previous night's fascination had left her husband's side, and was now clinging to his arm and whispering, "You left so suddenly – you missed all the fun. We went skinny dipping until dawn." Dennis is not a dummy, he has a modicum of awareness, and he definitely questioned the logic of skinny-dipping with a wife when the husband is 6-8 and weighs over 300 pounds. The wife continued to whisper all the unmentionable atrocities that they could have committed if he and that cute Whitney hadn't been so scared.

"You know sweetie, this is Southern California, nobody cares what happens after dark, surely not my husband," said the wife as she walked back to her husband's side.

The whole trip to Southern California was a disaster. Whitney should have beaten Pancho. Dennis and Whitney missed a bunch of fun the previous night, and to add insult to injury – Pancho told Whitney that his grandmother had a better overhead.

- CHAPTER 15 -

Best of Friends Continued: Art Larsen

"Unsophisticated, flaky, eccentric, and totally original" was the description of Art Larsen by Bud Collins in one of his columns. Sound vaguely familiar? Art Larsen first appeared in the world rankings in 1950 at No. 3 behind Budge Patty and Frank Sedgman – the same year he won the U.S. Championships. He was subsequently ranked No. 9 in 1951 and No. 9 again in 1954. He was ranked No. 1 in 1950 by the USLTA, and remained in the USLTA top ten until 1956. Art was small, somewhat of a ladies man, and possessed magnificent touch. He was inducted into the Tennis Hall of Fame in 1969.

Phil Garlington, the tennis coach at College of the Pacific, recruited Art to play college tennis. Phil's description of Art was interesting. Instead of "flaky" and "unsophisticated," his adjectives of choice were "aggressive" and "contemplative." He felt that Art was dedicated to the game and very bright. Phil had Art as a student in English at COP, consequently his assessment of Larsen's academic penchant was based on that expertise.

Whitney may have fashioned his style after the ebullient Larsen. Both players loved to play tennis for the drama. Whitney and Larsen believed that they were thespians and the tennis court was a stage where they practiced their craft. Both were entertainers, and when the curtain fell at the end of each match, they felt grieved and isolated. Both players hated to see a match end. There are hundreds of stories where they extended matches at the risk of losing just to experience another joy of the perfect volley or the perfect lob.

- CHAPTER 16 -

Best of Friends Continued: Jack Darrah, Pancho Gonzalez, Gene Scott

Whitney has maintained a friendship with Jack Darrah since high school. Jack played tennis for Albany High at the same time Whitney played at Alameda High. They met on the courts a few times in high school during league play. Whitney was a better player and won all the encounters, but he was supposed to: He was a nationally-ranked junior. Jack was a good athlete; he played football, basketball, and baseball. Tennis didn't become a serious pursuit until he was almost 30. By contrast, Whitney's entire athletic interest was tennis, and he was something of a prodigy.

Jack tells a story in connection with the 1949 Interscholastic Tennis Championships in Carmel. Jack was fortunate; he was just good enough to get his high school to pop for a trip to Carmel. He and two other players drove all the way to Carmel. In those days there were no freeways, so it was a feat to negotiate all the small towns from Albany to Monterey Bay. They had a little trouble in San Leandro where they were caught speeding. Fortunately, Art Larsen's dad was a city cop, and when the police saw the tennis racquets, the boys got off with a warning of sorts. The cops made the boys run wind sprints along the highway. Quite a contrast with present day police procedure; today, they would have spent the night in the slammer and faced the indignity of meeting their parents in the morning.

They finally made it to Carmel only to discover that Jack drew Whitney in the first round. Jack had visions of a three-set victory. An incredible match fought to the last point. As it turned out, Whitney won easily in straight sets. The same story was played out in doubles. Jack and his partner lost, also in straight sets.

The boys were out of the tournament in one day. Prudently, they should have hopped in the car and left for home, but they were 15 years old (except the driver, he was 18) and Carmel was teeming with teenage girls – a lethal combination that no respectable teenage boy could pass up. They decided to stay.

The Asilomar was a camp/hotel used by every institution on the West Coast for conferences. It was on the beach in Carmel, constructed of wood and bleached by the sea air. It gave a new meaning to the term rustic. The living quarters varied from individual rooms to dorm-like sleeping porches.

If you played in the tournament and didn't live in the Monterey area, and wanted an inexpensive place to stay, the Asilomar was the place. Jack and his friends had enough money for two nights, and they decided to stay for three. Normally that wouldn't present a problem; the Asilomar is not the Hilton. All you need to do is leave a window open for late night ingress and be sure to hit the road before the caretaker checks in the morning.

Carmel is not the jet-set playground of the Pacific Coast; midnight is a stretch for any activity worth pursuing. Jack and his friends did their very best; they searched for playmates up and down Ocean Avenue until only a cool, drizzly fog remained on the streets of Carmel. Stimulated by the pursuit, and thrilled as only a teenager can be, they ambled back to the Asilomar, crawled through the opened window, and barricaded the door with furniture to insure against a hostile caretaker. The boys were asleep by 1 a.m.

Jack was a talker; to this day Jack is a talker. He's articulate and tells great stories. If you are lucky enough to play doubles with him, prepare for extended, delightful chats during the crossovers. He has played doubles with Pancho Gonzalez, and has a win over Whitney and Don Kirbow. He was the captain of the Junior Davis Cup Team for years, and he is truly a Who's Who of tennis. However, at the Asilomar in 1949, his penchant for garrulous behavior almost got the boys busted. As it happened, the caretaker made his rounds earlier than usual that morning, and when he heard Jack talking in his sleep all hell broke loose. The caretaker, being a responsible sort, went ballistic. He attacked the barricaded door with a vengeance not seen in Carmel until Clint Eastwood made "Play Misty for Me."

Jack and his friends grabbed their gear and dove through the window just as the caretaker came crashing through the bedroom door. The boys landed in the sand and darted down the side of the dorm, laughing like crazy people. As they were about to make a final sprint for the car, a window opened from one of the adjoining rooms, and out flew Whitney. "Geez! Jack, can't you even sleep without talking?" Whitney said in his soft, slurry voice.

With the sounds of crashing furniture in the background, everyone piled into the car and headed for the tennis courts to watch Whitney win the tournament.

Requiem for a Heavyweight – Gene Scott

When Whitney woke up one morning in 1961 and discovered he was the No. 1 one player in the U.S., image was the first thing that popped into his brain. He needed a new image. Since everyone in the tennis world considered Jack Kramer the quintessential stroker in the game, Whitney decided to emulate Jack's strokes. He practiced extending his backswing and follow-through holding the pose in front of the mirror in his parents' living room.

He called Jack Frost and announced that the new Whitney Reed was about to take the court against all competition. No. 1 in the U.S., and with new and improved Jack Kramer strokes, No. 1 in the world was a distinct possibility.

The first tournament on the agenda, and the first tournament to see the new Whitney Reed, was an eight-man round-robin in Philadelphia. Whitney was scheduled to play Gene Scott in the first round.

Whitney really liked Gene Scott, and from all accounts, Gene was a very nice fellow. Gene's father was richer than God, it seems Gene's grandfather invented Pyrex and was the president of Owen Glass Works. Gene went to Yale and Virginia Law School, while Whitney went to Modesto JC and San Jose State. Ironically, with such diverse backgrounds, Whitney and Gene were very good friends.

Anyway, the tournament in Philly was to be Whitney's coming out – new game, new attitude – and Gene was the first player to benefit from transformation. Gene beat the pants off of Whitney. It wasn't even close, Gene's nice serve-and-volley game was too much for Whitney's Jack Kramer look-a-like game.

Gene must have felt some empathy for Whitney because he invited Whitney out to Long Island for an extended stay, and then named his Labrador retriever Whitney.

Requiem for the Lionhearted – Pancho Gonzalez

We all have our heroes, our idols. People we come across who possess some mysterious chemistry that causes our hearts to palpitate, our breath to catch in our throats, and our hand to become sweaty. We relish the time in their presence, but live in dread of saying or doing something that may alienate them. We feel less articulate when in their presence, and our self-confidence is as low as a .200 hitter. We try and impress these people at every opportunity, most of the time failing miserably. Usually these people possess something we truly admire, great intellectual capacity, great humanitarian feats, or great athletic ability.

It is not just their abilities; it is the intangible connection that happens when you catch a glimpse on the freeway of the perfect woman. The woman you know in your heart that under different circumstances, you could spend your life with, and when she takes the next off-ramp, you feel as though your heart has been ripped out.

Fortunately, as human beings, hero worshiping doesn't occur often. Oh, we may have bouts of instant admiration, but all-out, unadulterated hero worship does not happen that frequently. Frank Kovacs and possibly Art Larsen may have influenced Whitney early on. Frank Kovacs was a true character in the Whitney tradition, a fabulous player who never got the credit he deserved. Some of the anecdotes credited to Whitney could have easily been credited to Frank Kovacs. Whitney may have had a few more admirers because he was likeable with no discernable dark side. If Whitney took off his clothes and jumped in the pool, people would laugh and say Whitney was being Whitney. If Frank or Art pulled the same stunt, someone would have called the vice squad.

Whitney's relationship with Pancho Gonzalez was a little different. Where Whitney may have emulated Frank and Art to some extent, he revered Pancho. Of course, Pancho was a legend when Whitney was playing Kalamazoo. When Whitney beat Donald Dell in the NCAA finals, Pancho was the major attraction on the Jack Kramer's pro tour.

Pancho's tennis career is legendary. Born in 1928 in East LA, Gonzalez had a tough time in his early years dealing with intolerance. While Whitney may have experienced a little discrimination for being a tennis player in a redneck community like Alameda, it was nothing compared to what Pancho had to endure. Whitney had to deal with hiding his racquet on the way to school. Pancho had to deal with hiding from discrimination, bigotry, and Perry Jones.

Pancho had a reputation as a ruthless player on the tennis court. He wanted to win at any cost. He drove Whitney to distraction more than once, and a player driving Whitney to distraction is as unlikely as Wally Cox beating Rick Barry one-on-one. Conversely, once off the court Pancho could be exceedingly charming, and he was perplexed when one of the recipients of his outrageous behavior was still upset in the bar after a match. Pancho's credo, according to Whitney, was "all's fair in love, war, and competitive tennis." Once the war was over it was time for wine, women, and song.

No one was exempt from experiencing the rage within Pancho Gonzalez, not his opponents, not his doubles partners, and not his wives. Yet, Pancho seemingly had a soft spot for Whitney Reed. Whitney and Pancho's tennis careers merged when Al Bunis formed the Grand Masters Tour, and in 1978 Pancho proved what a good friend he could be.

Pancho took great delight in pointing out some of the deficiencies in Whitney's game: an overhead similar to his grandmother's, a serve similar to his wife's, and the goofiest looking backhand in tennis.

With all of Pancho Gonzalez's idiosyncrasies, he solidified his friendship in Whitney's heart with an unabashed act of kindness.

In 1978 the playoffs for the Grand Master's Tour were held in Greenbrier, White Sulphur Springs, W.Va. The Greenbrier is one of the most beautiful vacation spots in the world. Nestled in the forests and mountains of West Virginia, Greenbrier is old-world splendor with a Jack Nicklaus-designed golf course. Owens-Illinois was the generous sponsor, and they spared no expense. The players were treated like royalty: beautiful rooms, open bar, and hot and cold running barmaids. Well, maybe not hot and cold running barmaids, but there was always a gaggle of pretty and available woman around Greenbrier.

Whitney was always a bit careless with his colorful rhetoric. He would mumble something that could be construed as harmless or, if you listened closely, it could be construed as a little blue in color. For example, when he said to a girlfriend of a fellow player, "I liked to peed my pants," when the girlfriend blushed, he immediately corrected himself and said, "I liked the Pirates of Penzance." And that was 15 years before "Pretty Woman."

All the Grand Masters were required to say a few words before dinner. Traditionally, the players would thank the sponsors, thank the Greenbrier, and praise God for giving them wonderful athletic genes. The speeches were so predictable that almost everyone stifled yawns, reached for drinks, and tried desperately to keep from nodding off. When it was Whitney's turn, everyone perked up; because you had to listen closely to be sure you heard what you think you heard. Whitney may say, "pass me a glass" and when it's delivered to an unsuspecting audience, it may appear to sound like, "pain in the ass."

Unfortunately, that's exactly what happened in 1978. Whitney was giving his required talk at dinner. Whether he muttered, mumbled, or growled something that sounded like "pass me a glass" it was interpreted as "pain in the ass." How it got misconstrue to reflect Whitney's opinion of the wife of the president of Owens-Illinois is anyone's guess. Nevertheless, the president of Owens-Illinois, to this day, is convinced that Whitney called his wife, in a room full of famous tennis players, celebrities, and captains of industry, a pain in the ass.

If the Grand Masters Tour was still being played, and if Greenbrier was still the venue, Whitney Reed would still be persona-non-grata. If Whitney was the No. 1 one player in the universe, and if he beat Roger Federer at this year's Wimbledon, he would still be person-non-grata at Greenbrier.

So in 1978, how did Pancho Gonzalez react to Whitney's being debarred from the following years playoffs? He told Al Bunis to take Greenbrier and all it's trappings and, to paraphrase, "put it where the sun don't shine." Pancho played the Grand Masters Tour in 1979, but he frequently mentioned the unfair treatment of Whitney Reed to the press, and refused to take advantage of the easy living at the Greenbrier.

Whether Pancho was displaying an overt act of loyalty, or engaging in a little play war with the Grand Masters Tour, is conjecture, but the fact that Pancho was extremely loyal to those he considered valuable was not conjecture.

Pancho was an enigma; he detested people for reasons only he was aware of, and he had a genuine affection for people he felt were worthy. Whitney was worthy, and most of the tennis world was not. Sometimes people would cross over from the detested to the worthy. Jim Nelson was ready to duke it out with Pancho over a disputed call, and later in life, Pancho praised Jim to the moon for beating Gordon Davis in the finals of the 45s.

He had running feuds with almost every level of tennis authority – beginning with Perry Jones, who singlehandedly kept him out of junior tennis, cumulating with his legendry money feuds with Jack Kramer. According to a several reliable sources, the money feuds where well-founded, and the basic reason there was so much acrimony between Pancho and the rest of the tennis world. Pancho was the world professional champion and Jack Kramer paid more money to Tony Trabert as a rookie on the tour. It would be like paying the No. 1 draft pick more money than Michael Jordan. Athletes are incredibly proud people, and when you add to the mix race, money, and respect, the situation becomes extremely volatile. It's no wonder Pancho spent the last years of his life as one pissed-off individual.

Pancho lived about four different lives. He retired, returned, retired, and returned. At age 43 he beat Jimmy Connors in the Pacific Southwest Championships in Los Angeles. Jimmy was 19. A year later he beat Charlie Pasarell in the most famous match ever played at Wimbledon. As a senior, Pancho played doubles with Whitney on occasion. Whitney says they had lots in common: gambling, smoking, drinking, chasing women, poker, backgammon, bizarre behavior at times, loyalty, honesty, and an absolute love and respect for the game.

When Whitney got old, he lost to a hematologist from La Grand, Oregon, a postal clerk from Merced, and a firefighter from Fresno. Pancho did Whitney one better; when he got old he lost to a garbage man from Alviso. Mind you, they hated to lose as much as they hated boredom, but the fact is, the aging pair wouldn't care if they lost to a pair of transgenders from the Castro as long as the effort included a ball, racquet, a net, and someone on the other side of the court to compete with.

Now Whitney is older and Pancho is gone. If Whitney's life ended today, the Chronicle obituary writer could say he lived life to the fullest, he did it his way, and none of his ex-wives hated him. In Pancho's case, the epitaph is more complex. Notwithstanding his contribution to tennis, his charisma, and his great athletic ability, he was an angry person and he died too soon.

- CHAPTER 17 -

Unforgettable Characters: Jack Frost

Forgive the redundancy, but discovering why a bunch of athletes would run, walk, and crawl from one tournament to another for silver cups is a mesmerizing phenomenon. Why these players begged promoters for traveling money to play tennis in Oslo, or why a couple of them bought a beat-up jalopy for a one-way trip to Forest Hills was an amazement. Some of the players cut short educations and left brides on the courthouse steps, and some like Whitney even got paper routes just to bat a little white ball around.

Jack Frost said it best: Tour players of Whitney's era had life all figured out. They realized that they were the luckiest people on the planet. No matter what life had in store, when they opened their eyes in the morning their very existence was the best it ever was going to be. Whitney came to this realization sometime around his 13th birthday, and he never once considered another option. He just lived his life with a slight grin on his face, because he knew it couldn't get any better.

The picture of Whitney, Cliff Mayne, Jack Darrah, and Norm Peterson (vintage 1946) on page – sitting on a net in Sacramento may have been the moment. They may have turned, looked at each other and thought simultaneously: Wow! Tennis is the key to life.

It may have been an epiphany of sorts, or maybe a knock on the head. One day they are in a classroom fighting to stay awake, and the next day they are on a plane heading for Wimbledon. When you're young, time has little meaning, so there may have been a small interlude between the classroom, Berkeley Tennis Club, Wimbledon, and the realization that they were the luckiest people on the planet, but who's counting.

However it happened or whatever metaphysical quirk in the universe occurred, Whitney and all the other players were anointed. They had access to the most exclusive neighborhoods in the world – Newport, South Hampton, Monte Carlo. They traveled around the world as most people go to the grocery store. They played with the rich, the famous, and the infamous. How much money would a person need to earn to live that life – about as much as Bill Gates does? No wonder, every morning Jack and Whitney thank providence for every gene they inherited, every exceptional piece of muscle tissue in their bodies, and the little synapses in their brain that made it all possible, and if there is a tennis god, they'd thank her too.

They bought their ticket with talent, and that's what the rich and famous wanted – to be associated and rub shoulders with great talent. Whitney and the anointed few were exposed to the best life had to offer, and all they needed to do was show up at some of the most expensive real estate on the planet and play a silly little game.

Jack Frost figured it out around the same time as Whitney. One day Jack was beating the crap out of some kid on a playground in Monterey, and six months later he was beating the crap out of some kid on a tennis court in Pebble Beach. The only difference was instead of a black eye, Jack's opponent got a bruised ego.

Although they were fierce competitors, Jack and Whitney shared a bond of mutual understanding and affection. Jack was traditional and smart as a whip. Whitney was an iconoclast and smart as a whip. So it wasn't the attraction of the opposites that sustained their friendship, more like a genuine feeling of mutual fascination. Whitney enjoyed Jack's gymnastic mind, and Jack waited in wonderment to see what Whitney would do next.

Whitney may have gotten a perverse pleasure from subjecting Jack to his world. What Whitney didn't understand was that Jack, in fact, did understand Whitney's world and reveled in it. Consequently, years later, when Whitney gave Jack a call and invited him to spend a weekend at his place, Jack couldn't pack his bags fast enough.

Jack, as mentioned, was very smart. Smart as in - today I think I'll learn Swahili kind of smart. Consequently, it took Jack about a New York minute to figure out that the chances of sleeping in a bed over the weekend were slim and none. Further, the chances of actually sleeping were equally remote.

- CHAPTER 18 -

Something's Rotten
In China

The plan was to meet at Pier 7 in San Francisco sometime between 8 p.m. and midnight. Jack showed up at 8 p.m. sharp. Whitney was behind the bar pouring beer to a varied cliental. A few Montgomery Street types and a bunch of rowdy dock workers. What they all had in common was Whitney. He was everyone's best friend. The guy in the three-piece suit had the same standing as the guy in Levi's and a flannel shirt. Everyone had a drink, and everyone looked very contented.

When Whitney saw Jack he slipped out from behind the bar and greeted him with a cold beer and a promise of a fun weekend. The promise came in the form of a few guttural remarks that Jack interpreted as, "Gee, Jack, it's really good to see you."

Jack was under no illusion; if Whitney were involved, the weekend would be anything but boring. He found a comfortable spot at the end of the bar and watched the patrons and the bartender at work.

Through out the evening a Runyonesque gallery of patrons flowed in and out of Pier 7. Terrific-looking women from the financial district out for a quick drink before embarking on a late-night date, and married men looking for a one-evening stand before heading home to Walnut Creek or Ross. Finally, a few people drifted by just to enjoy Whitney's company.

Periodically someone would stray over to Jack's spot and strike up a conversation. When a strayee discovered that Jack was Whitney's old friend, the game of Ping Pong became the topic of conversation. Jack soon was aware that the latest chapter in the ever-evolving Whitney mystique was his celebrated proficiency at Ping Pong. Jack knew all about Whitney and Ping Pong, and, as a dedicated reader of Herb Caen, he had caught Herb's opus on Whitney's willingness to take on all comers in at Pier 7.

What the everyday waterfront player/patron didn't understand was how extraordinary Whitney's ability was to play a game that required hand-eye coordination. His coordination compares with that of Mike Schmidt or Brooks Robinson. (I use comparisons to fit the time frames.) The difference is Mike Schmidt and Brooks Robinson played a game that paid a buck. They didn't need, in their later years, to hustle a dollar playing Ping Pong.

The problem that all the weekend jocks had was in Whitney's appearance. He didn't look like a world-class athlete. Six feet, one inch, red-rimmed eyes, skinny legs and arms, the outer shell was no Jose Canseco. It isn't difficult to imagine the average guy bellying up to the bar thinking that the few summers of Ping Pong at Cal Camp qualified him to challenge Whitney to play for money. From Whitney's perspective, it was a lot like stealing without the anxiety of breaking the law.

Around 1:30 a.m. there was no relief in the number of people entering the bar, no one was watching the time, and no one seemed tired, least of all Whitney. At about five minutes to two, a little undercurrent of anticipation occurred. Whitney was behind the bar polishing glasses, draining ice bins, and generally preparing to close the bar. A couple of guys started to maneuver a large board and wrestle it over the pool table. Out of a closet came a bag of goodies: paddles, nets, and connecting hardware. Within minutes, the Ping Pong table was set up and ready for action.

All up and down the bar people were slipping off stools and reaching for their wallets. Lots of money suddenly appeared on the tables. A large black board was propped up behind the bar and Whitney wrote down names starting with a number 1 and finishing with a number 12. By 2:20 all the doors were barred and the windows were covered, four players, two at each table, were furiously banging Ping Pong balls back and forth like little white tracer bullets. Every so often someone would swear and slam a paddle on the table and storm off. Whitney would peal off a few bills and pay the player remaining.

The constabularies in San Francisco prescribed to the theory of live and let live as long as no one bitched. The fact was that many Ping Pong players made their living fighting fires and protecting the peace. Consequently late- night Ping Pong was fun and worry-free as long as everyone played by the rules.

On the night of Jack's visit, an exceptional number of people were left in Pier 7 after 2 a.m. If Whitney was concerned, it didn't show. He kept the games going and the money moving from one participant to another.

Jack was watching everyone, especially a tall Asian guy who seemed to be watching only Whitney. The Asian guy was alone, sitting on a stool with his back against the bar. He had on a blue warm-up outfit with a parrot stitched over the heart. On his feet was a pair of very expensive tennis shoes. He looked like a 6-foot-3 Jet Li.

Whitney's demeanor is so dispassionate and so blasé that it is difficult for most people to discern what a responsive and insightful person exists under all that attitude. Jack was one of the few people that Whitney has allowed a glimpse of his complex personality. They had spent more than one evening sipping Jim Beam and discussing the cosmos. So to Jack, Whitney's concern for Jack's bar time comfort was not out of character. Jack knew that for Whitney to enjoy himself he needed to know that everyone was sharing the adventure.

Jack was actually having a great time. The simple act of people-watching was worth the admission. Besides Jack is an affable and a very loquacious fellow, he had very little trouble finding stimulating conversation, and there were all those great-looking women to appreciate.

The attractive females notwithstanding, Jack was fascinated with the Asian fellow. He just kept starring at Whitney. When finally Whitney reluctantly agreed to play someone, the Asian guy nearly fell off the stool trying to get closer to the table.

Whitney's first Ping Pong match was calculatingly close. One of the local hotshots was trying to win his first game ever against Whitney. The guy didn't have a clue. Whitney would let him get a glimpse of victory then snatch it away at the last minute. If they had been playing pool, it would have been obvious that Whitney was hustling the guy.

Andy Anderson, the owner of Pier 7 at the time, figured out pretty fast that backing Whitney was a good deal. Andy would place side bets or just back Whitney outright. The deal was good for Whitney and very good for Andy.

Whitney first noticed the Asian fellow when he replaced the net after a rather heated exchange between a longshoreman and a Montgomery Street type. Nothing violent, the Montgomery type was a little mad and a paddle slipped out of his hand and knocked a stanchion loose. Whitney noticed a gym bag on the floor as he was tightening the net. When he looked up, the Asian guy was so close to the table that he was practically drooling on the plywood. So in a sign language, hand waving, and some table pounding as means of communication, Whitney asked the guy if he wanted to play. The guy was so happy he almost cried. Andy was so happy when he heard that the Asian fellow wanted to play for money, he almost cried.

The first game was for $10, and Whitney won 21-19. The Asian guy played well but was not very steady. A lot of his smashes were a little wild. The next game, also for $10, went about the same as the first. Whitney won 21-17.

Andy Anderson was beside himself. He pulled Whitney to one side and begged him to raise the bet. Whitney had not just fallen off the turnip truck; he had hustled enough backgammon, bowling, and gin rummy to smell a con. However, it was Andy's money, and maybe the guy was just what he appeared to be – a fairly good Ping Pong player. Whitney suppressed his concern and Game 3 was played for $50. The Asian guy played great for 40 points. Whitney would jump ahead a few points, then his opponent would catch up. At 20-all, Whitney served out the game. The Asian guy threw a fifty-dollar bill on the table.

Andy walked over and whispered something in the ear of the Asian guy. Whitney was puzzled. Andy was like many indigent San Franciscans, an American who struggled with English as a primary language. Andy spoke a version of Pier 7 bar talk that occasionally even the locals found hard to understand. Even Whitney wasn't sure what Andy was saying most of the time. Nonetheless, Andy communicated with the 6-3 Asian like he was a long lost brother.

Five minutes of conversation and both participants were smiling like they just got a date with Angelina Jolie. Andy sauntered over, slapped Whitney on the back, and announced that the next game was double or nothing.

The double or nothing game was scripted pretty much along the same lines of the $50 game. Whitney jumped out to a modest lead. The Asian guy missed a few easy putaways, but kept the score close. The Asian guy reached 20 first; Whitney battled to tie the score and then go up by one with the Asian guy serving at 22-23. The Asian stepped back from the table and took a huge swing at the ball, it responded like an ICBM. If Whitney hadn't been in the way the ball would have reached the bay. As it was, the ball hit Whitney on the shoulder and bounced into the crowd. Whitney and Andy were up $100.

The Asian apologized all over the place. He practically prostrated himself in front of Andy pleading for another game. All he wanted was a chance of redemption, a chance to save face. (The translation of all these histrionics was pure conjecture; no one was sure what the guy was trying to communicate. He may have been apologizing, or he may have been worried that Whitney may want to call it a night.) Whatever the interpretation, Andy could care less about saving face, or if the Asian was suffering a form of esoteric Eastern anxiety. The Asian was a pigeon, and Whitney was the tool to do the plucking. He could smell a nice addition to the night's take.

All this communication occurred much to Whitney's amazement. He knew Andy was not "Mr. Communication" and, as far as Whitney was aware, the Asian only spoke a singsong form of Oriental gibberish. Yet the purpose was obvious, another game for another double or nothing. Amazing how easy it is to communicate when money is the objective.

Whitney felt that he had entered Ping Pong paradise. Everything he hit was a winner. The Asian was good and made some spectacular shots, but in the end it was Whitney 21-17. After the game and after the initial euphoria had dissipated, Whitney got a familiar feeling, the feeling he got after he playing backgammon with Jack Darrah. He beat Darrah a couple of

times back in the '60s, since then he had lost so many games
that he felt that he had underwritten Jack's expenses on the tour.

Andy had no such feeling; he left $200 on the bar and
raised one finger in the air. The Asian responded with a smile
and a nod.

Interpreting Andy and the Asian's enthusiasm as one more
double of nothing game, Whitney took a sip of beer and
reluctantly settled in, not so confidently, for another round
of Ping Pong.

Whitney jumped out to a 10-5 lead. The Asian closed to 11-8.
Whitney hit a series of terrific smashes and led 18-14 when the
Asian smacked a couple of cross-table winners to tie the score.
The score bounced back in forth neither player showing an
advantage. At 27-all and the Asian serving, Whitney missed an
easy return, and five seconds latter the Asian whacked a vicious
slam for the game. The Asian picked up his money and headed
for the door. Immediately the crowd groaned; the quality of Ping
Pong had been stupendous and they wanted to see more.

Andy was off his perch at the bar in a flash. He caught
the Asian guy just as he was opening the front door. A couple
of conspiratorial whispers and the two disappeared onto
the Embarcadero.

Jack and Whitney chatted awhile about fun times, big wins,
and lusty women tennis players. They talked about the best
serve, best forehand, and the cutest legs. Laura Lou Jahn and
Mary Ann Mitchell won all the important categories, and
Althea Gibson won for the best serve and best volley.

After what seemed like an eternity to the rambunctious
crowd, Andy and the Asian guy returned to the bar. This time
the atmosphere was not as sunny. Andy's I-just-got-a-date-

with-Angelina-Jolie morphed into I-just-got-a-date- with-Miss-Marple. The look the Asian guy had was, I just got a date with Angelina Jolie,

Andy took an uncharacteristic deep breath and announced to the crowd that one final game was worth $500.

Whitney almost fell off the stool. He had a really bad feeling about the Asian guy. He saw the gleam in the eye of the Asian when he hit the last smash to even the score, and he noticed how slowly the Asian picked up the money and started for the door.

Jack laughed, and whispered in Whitney's ear, "I hope Andy isn't using his own money."

Whitney didn't even waste time trying to dissuade Andy from the ridiculous bet. He simply walked over to the table and picked up his paddle.

The Asian smiled over the net, tossed Whitney the ball and said in pure idiomatic English, "Your serve."

Whitney saw the ball when it left his hand on the first serve. He saw the ball again somewhere between the ninth and tenth point. Andy saw the five hundred dollars vanish out the door clutched in the hands of a smiling Asian. Jack thanked the all-mighty that he decided to take Whitney up on his invitation, because this tale would be impossible to retell in the vivid imagery it deserved.

Eventually Andy and Whitney established the origin of the ethereal Asian guy. He was either the third-ranked Ping Pong player in the world, or the third-ranked Ping Pong player in Taiwan. It didn't make much difference in the scheme of things. What Whitney and Andy did agree on was that Herb Caen should pay one-half the $500.

- CHAPTER 19 -

Jack Sprat Could Eat No Fat

.

On a different level, Jack Frost's life was every bit as fascinating as Whitney's. Both players knew early on that tennis life was the panacea of the world, and both dreaded the day when they actually had to face reality. Jack was born in Monterey, California. His father was a building contractor and his mother a homemaker. Jack was a very good high school athlete. He played football, basketball, and a lot of baseball. In fact, around Monterey High School Jack was Mr. Jock.

Tennis began on the playground of a local grammar school. Some kid said something about being able to beat the pants off Jack in tennis. To Jack, tennis was a sissy sport, but a challenge is a challenge, so he trudged up the hill to the tennis courts in back of the high school. Jack didn't even know how to hold a racquet, but he had the athletic ability to run down balls and somehow bat them back over the net. He beat the kid. Jack was 10 years old. Two years later, Leo Kohler, the pro at Pebble Beach, told Jack that he could go east next year. Jack looked perplexed and asked, "Tennis in Salinas?" "No," said Leo, "The nationals." For an Irish kid who enjoyed fighting Sicilian kids for a chance to get a few at-bats at the park in Monterey, this was an amazing change of athletic pace.

The first tournament he entered he won; he got his name in the papers. They handed him a trophy, and a couple of the girls in the stands giggled and flirted with him. He knew he had died and gone to prepubescent heaven.

As mentioned earlier, Jack and Whitney discovered early on that all they need to do to join Art Larsen and Budge Patty on the Riviera was to keep winning tennis tournaments. The Northern California level of competition was a little stiffer, the Country Club kids were a little better, but all the really great athletes found other pursuits. Fortunately, for Jack and

Whitney, Frank Robinson became a baseball player, John Brodie became a football player, and Vada Pinson decided playing baseball was almost as fun as chasing girls, and there was more money in it.

Jack's dad wanted him to be the next Babe Ruth, but Jack saw tennis as the highway to heaven.

Jack elected an atypical circuitous route after tennis. He graduated from Stanford, went into a masters program, and eventually took a doctorate in history. He won a Fulbright scholarship and wound up in the Sudan where he co-authored a book on the politics of the area.

More rumors abound around Jack's early years then Angelina Jolie's love life. Jack Darrah is certain that Jack was a spy during the Cold War – a true- life "I Spy." It is true, Jack had an enigmatic relationship with the State Department; that little tidbit of information came from Jack personally.

He was asked to coach the Ghanaian National Tennis Team. Jack took off for Africa to coach a team virtually talent-free. The team had lost so many matches and had become so complacent that Kwame Nkrumah, the George Washington of Africa, who had no fondness for Americans, decided his team needed to reflect the philosophy of his reign. They needed to endure a transformation. Kwame wanted, for obvious reasons, his team to become winners. Jack ignored the "good old boy" attitude surrounding the team, and recruited athletes. He had all these kids hitting deep approach shots, racing to the net and putting away forehand volleys. The team wasn't the 1960 U.S. Olympic hockey team, or the 1969 Mets, but they won their share of games. Kwame was pleased and decided Jack was one of the "handsome Americans."

Subsequently, Jack moved to Europe for 3 1/2 years and did all kinds of mysterious things. Jack eventually chose to take a job as the head pro at the Eldorado Country Club in Indian Wells, California. He retired in 2004.

- Chapter 20 -

Unforgettable Characters Revisited: Jim Nelson

Jim Nelson was the sixth man on the USC tennis team in 1955. He was a good tennis player, quick and very steady. By today's sophisticated computer rankings, he would probably be ranked somewhere in the top 3000 players in the U.S. Jim would have had a difficult time breaking into the elite circle of tournaments. If he shot off a letter to Wimbledon and asked for a couple of bucks to cover traveling expenses, they would have choked on their crumpets.

Now Jim is one of the elite senior players in the country. He's one of those rare athletes who have actually improved with age. As a senior, Jim has wins over players he used to watch on television. One of the more exciting wins was at the Sun Hill Racquet Club in 1987; Nelson and Jim Pugh beat Whitney and Don Kierbow 6-0, 6-1.

According to Nelson, Don and Whitney showed up for the match a half-hour late, and they were so spent from the previous night that during the warm-up they could barely keep the ball in play. Kiebrow, once described by Jack Kramer as the dark horse of tennis, was comatose; balls were bouncing off everything but the strings on his racquet. Whitney fared a little better, having more experience in playing under trying circumstances.

"We would have had a very difficult time if Whitney and Don had not chosen to spend the night in Newport with a couple of blondes," said Jim after the match.

"A win is a win," said Whitney after the match.

"What match?" said Don after the match.

Jim Nelson has won 90 plus gold balls. This means 90 times he has been victorious in a national tournament. All this success happened after Jim reached his 35th birthday. Jim never played a senior doubles final against Jon Douglas, Butch

Bucholz, Barry MacKay, or Dennis Ralston. Barry MacKay became a promoter extraordinaire; Dennis coached the Davis Cup team for a while, and Jon became the best real estate broker on the planet. With the exception of Pancho Gonzalez and Whitney, very few great younger players matured to be great older players.

Jim and Lenny Linborg, his long time doubles partner, are a kick to watch. Lenny is a great big guy with huge hands and Titanium knees. He lumbers to the net and volleys like Pete Sampras. Jim plays with this huge Weed racquet and lobs like Whitney Reed. They are a formidable team.

Jim's chosen vocation is stockbrokering. For Jim, it was job made in heaven. He has all the tools; he's charming, smart, and tenacious – tenacious being the operative word for anyone in that business, and anyone interested in winning at the senior level.

Jim Nelson is such a great interview, he so forthcoming, all I needed to do was to open the discussion with, "Tell me some funny Whitney stories." The whole book could have been entitled, "Reflections of Whitney Reed as seen through the eyes of Jim Nelson." At lunch, I asked Jim if he had any one incident that could define Whitney as a player. He needed about a 30 seconds of thought and 10 minutes to tell me the tale of the Canadian finals in 1960.

He and Cliff Mayne had just finished a doubles match. They had a decision to make, watch Whitney in the finals or catch a plane for home. When they saw Whitney stagger onto the court, the decision was obvious. They grabbed a couple of beers and settled in to watch the show.

Canadian Championships 1960

Whitney's performance in the 1960 Canadian National Championship resembled Bevo Francis going one-on-one with Connie Hawkins. (If you can't relate to that metaphor, you are too young for this book). Whitney's opponent was the Canadian National Junior Champion. A player young, vital, and about as fit as those guys who model men's underwear.

The finals were played at noon, about 10 minutes after Whitney first responds to the light of day. During the warm-up, Whitney's opponent looked like a reincarnation of Ellsworth Vines. Whitney, in contrast, looked like the reincarnation of Harold Lloyd. Balls were bouncing off Whitney's frame like Midwest hail off of a cartop. The youngster ran all over place trying to return errant balls that kept flying off Whitney's racquet. If big Bill Tilden was watching from heaven, he'd think he was watching Pancho Gonzales playing a celebrity singles with Don Rickles.

The first set was a disaster. Whitney was so slow getting to the ball that even his uncanny touch failed to produce any rhythm. Whitney would lob and the kid would run it down. Whitney would drop shot and the kid would retrieve it and hit it back for a winner. Countless times in the first set, Whitney would come to the net only to watch a passing shot whiz by his nose on the way to a corner. The first set ended with Whitney missing his signature shot, a forehand half volley at the service line. The ball wasn't even close and neither was the score: 6-0.

This was Canada, not Newport, and Whitney couldn't get to a couple of beers to surreptitiously relieve the lingering effects of the night before. He had to wait for his body to metabolize whatever he ingested in the previous 12 hours. He remembered the ubiquitous blonde-haired person in sequins wanting to play poker for under apparel, and it pissed him off that he couldn't remember what happened. He remembered telling everyone within reach that tomorrow was the finals and he had to leave, and that may have been early in the evening. He had to focus. The kid was about to serve the first game of the second set, and he was not even sure his shoes were tied.

The junior champion was leading 3-0 in the second when Whitney felt the first stirrings of recovery. The sky looked a little bluer, the court a little sharper – he could actually see the lines on the other side of the net. In the fourth game, he won his serve. The pop off the racquet was beginning to sound like a real tennis player was holding the racquet. Thank God for good genes, he thought.

He knew in the fifth game that he had a chance at salvaging something from the match. The kid's serve was just as powerful, but he was returning it with a modicum of authority. Whitney followed a couple of second serves to the net and volleyed them back sharply. The kid missed two passing shots down the line and Whitney had a service break. Whitney held in the sixth game at love. Life was looking up, now if he could quit thinking about the blonde-haired woman in sequins, he may have a chance to pull this match off.

Both players held serve until 5-all. In the 11th game, Whitney hit two sharp service returns that the kid drilled back crosscourt for winners. At 30-love, the kid double-faulted out of nowhere. Whitney's nerves did a timeout; a familiar warm sensation filled his abdominal cavity. The next three points were vintage Reed. Whitney kept the ball in play forever. The kid ran to the net, ran to the baseline, ran to his left, and ran to his right chasing Whitney's looping crosscourt forehands and backhands. The kid would hit the ball at a 100 mph and Whitney would return it at 50 mph. Whitney's shots touched the lines and the kid's just missed. In the 12th game, Whitney held serve at love. At 7-5 the second set was history.

The third and final set started with a bang. The kid was a kid, he had the power of youth, and he ran for everything, but Whitney was finally in his rhythm. He served, strolled to the center of the court, and volleyed a ball that either dropped like a hard-boiled egg or flittered to the baseline like a butterfly. The ball seemed propelled by magic, and before anyone in the stands could take two sips of beer, the score was 3-1.

On the first point of the fifth game, the kid served to Whitney's backhand. The ball came back in a vicious slicing action, touching the outside line about three feet behind the service line. The kid got to the ball in plenty of time to drive it to the corner. A great shot if Whitney had tried to cover a down the line shot, but he didn't. He volleyed behind the kid. The junior champion skidded to a stop, reached back and hooked the ball up in the air in a short inadvertent lob. Any other player in the world would have charged like a lion and crushed the ball in the direction of downtown Toronto. Whitney charged like a lion, did a Satchel Page wind up and lobbed off a lob. The ball flew over the kid's head and dropped like a stone on the baseline. The kid turned, watched the ball land, and with a sigh of resignation, walked to the baseline.

The next three points were simple. The kid served like a banshee, and Whitney returned and kept the ball in play sometimes a little more than necessary. Amazingly, the kid continued to run down every ball, never did he let a ball go by without a valiant effort to make a return. When finally Whitney broke serve at 4-1, the kid, on the cross over, took a drink of water, wiped his face with a towel, and walked out to the baseline to receive serve.

Whitney looked across the net and prepared to serve. He tossed the ball and smoothly hit his serve in the direction of the kid's backhand. When he looked down, the Canadian Junior Champion was sitting on the court clutching his thigh. A second later, he rolled onto his back and pulled his thigh to his chest. Cramps had brought an unceremonious end to the match.

Whitney ran over to the kid and helped him to his feet. With his arm around his shoulder, Whitney guided the kid to the sideline chairs, and helped him massage away the cramp. The poor kid was in excruciating pain. Whitney patted him on the back, ruffled his hair, and whispered something in his ear.

To no one in particular, as he walked off the court, Whitney mumbled in his inimitable fashion: "A good boy, but the fuckin' kid has got to get in better shape."

- CHAPTER 21 -

Questions to Ponder for No Earthly Reason

A quandary that generates nagging, perplexing questions is: What makes a person pathologically pursue being the best tennis player in the world between the age of 10 and 30, and then after 30, morph into a television color person or a celebrity doubles partner? What makes a person consider suicide when he picks up the morning paper and his name is not prominently displayed on the front page of the sports section? How is it that one day a player is being interviewed by Bud Collins, and the next day his name is on a package of sure grip, or a dated pair of tennis shoes? How come some players go from No. 1 in the world of tennis to No. 1 trillion in the world of life?

Maybe it is a matter of more important pursuits – marriage, mortgages, and shoes for the kiddies. Maybe it is as simple as, been there, done that. The great player has proven he or she can win the big tournament, make the big shot.

Jack Frost feels that there is another element to the enigma. He feels that as the great players grow older, their skills erode. Conversely, mediocre players who have the time and energy to keep playing can sometimes develop their skills enough to surpass a player who has allowed the skills to diminish. Jack's contention is that it is a matter of ego. Jack Frost at 70 does not want too lose to a 40-year-old club player with a knee brace. Jack knows that the results will be in the local paper by morning, and every bar in town will have the story by cocktail hour – metaphorically speaking.

Maybe a deep thinker like Allen Fox can shed some light on this dilemma. I doubt that he'll say it's the money. If that's the case, Agassi would have retired years ago, he has about 20 dollars less than Bill Gates.

When I asked Whitney why some players quit and never play as seniors, his reaction was money. I was surprised. He didn't give it a moment's thought, it just popped out – money was the reason. Then I relayed a story I heard from a once-great player, who will remain anonymous, and I quote, "If you were a champion at 25 you don't need to be a champion at 65. Furthermore, I have found that life is not all about forehands, backhands, and computer rating."

When I finished my recital, Whitney looked aghast, I thought he was going to blow a gasket. He said that a player who didn't honor the game didn't deserve his or her God-given talent. He waved his arms, huffed and puffed, and looked off into the distance for an eternity and said, "Ted Williams would not want anything on his tombstone but 'baseball player', and Jerry Rice would not want anything on his tombstone but 'football player.' " In fact, he continued his tirade, "I'll probably die before you, so I'm telling you right now, when I pass on you put 'tennis performer' on my gravestone." Over the pass year, I've had a zillion conversations with Whitney, and I still can't anticipate what will set him off.

How does Jim Nelson feel about all this rhetoric? He's "happy as a pig in a poke." He has over 90 gold balls in his pocket.

- CHAPTER 22 -

Whitney is an Unforgettable Character

Whitney's point of view is simple: being a champion is fun, but being a performer is imperative; in his mind, one shouldn't exist without the other. Moreover, if you can't be a champion at 65, you surely can be a performer. Bottom line, Whitney received more satisfaction from sensing a crowd's admiration for his skills than standing on a platform with a fabricated smile, holding a trophy.

Whitney was never embarrassed on the tennis court, at least not because of age or eroding skills. He has been embarrassed by not performing in a manner he felt pleased the crowd, but never did that embarrassment foster anything but a few extra beers after a tough defeat. Many times, for one reason or another, he lost to players who shouldn't be allowed to carry his tennis bag, but he never quit the game. When some pediatrician beat him in Stockton, he chalked it up to lack of preparation. When he lost three and one to a painting contractor in Bakersfield his only regret was missing a behind-the-back volley in the fifth game of the second set. Ego never seemed to be Whitney's nemesis. He loved to win, but losing never led to quitting.

He was ranked in the top five most of his life. He's is a former No. 1- ranked player. He has played and beaten the best players of his time. He went five sets with Neal Fraser at Wimbledon. He beat Emerson, Laver, and Fraser on the Caribbean tour. Why didn't he look for something other than a paper route when time began to take its toll? I think the blame lies with the USTA (United States Tennis Association).

The USTA was formed to promote tennis, but doomed Whitney to a vagabond life. After the formation of the USTA, there were more tennis tournaments than you could shake a stick at, and when the Grand Masters Tour was formed it made Whitney feel like he had died and gone to tennis heaven. He had the unique opportunity to play tennis and make a buck to boot. He could continue to indulge in the most important things in his life – performing on a tennis court, and eating regularly.

Whitney continued to play seniors after the Grand Masters. He would have continued to play competitively if the only tour was in Peoria. As friends can attest, it doesn't take much to get Whitney on a tennis court. Don Pimley used to host the Hops Invitational, a round-robin tournament played on the Oakland public courts. Eight teams played 28 games; each team contributes a couple of bucks for beer and prize money. The object, obviously, was to win the money, but in the process, each team had to drink a beer after each game.

The year Whitney played, he showed up in the morning already beer in hand. When he saw Jim Nelson drinking a glass of milk before the first match, he cried foul. Whitney said coating the stomach with milk gave Jim an unfair advantage. The penalty was decided among the participants – Jim must chug two beers before the first match. Jim wasn't exactly clear on the final results the year Whitney played, but he remembers that Whitney drank most of the beer, and won all the money.

- CHAPTER 23 -

Davis Cup: Not All the Play Was On the Court
and
More Shoddy Thoughts

Whitney's Davis Cup career was interesting. He played well at times, but it was not a part of his tennis resume that he would choose to show his mom.

In 1958, Barry MacKay and Butch Bucholz, who would turn pro in 1961, were members of the Davis Cup Team that was captained by Perry Jones. Jones was strict, and invoked a curfew on his players. A curfew to Whitney was about as important as a diet soda after 9 p.m. To compound the felony, Jones had MacKay, Bucholz, and Whitney room together – a move comparable to housing the fox with the chickens.

McKay was ranked No. 1 in the U.S. Bucholz was ranked No. 3. Whitney was ranked No. 8. In terms of who had the most partying experience, Whitney was No. 1, MacKay No. 21 and Bucholz No. 251.

The 1958 edition of the Davis Cup America-Zone was held in Toronto, Canada. The U.S. team was matched against Canada. Perry Jones selected Whitney and Barry MacKay to play singles. Whitney won his match against Robert Bedard, and Barry won his match against Donald Fontana. Sam Giammalva and MacKay won the doubles to clinch the victory.

Whitney was introduced to a woman well-known in tennis society. To say they hit it off famously would be an understatement. They soon became an item off the court. The problem was, Davis Cup team members do not make a lot of money, so courting was a challenge. Although players did get a little money for expenses, it was not enough to pay for champagne picnics. Davis Cup players, unless they were independently wealthy, did not take their dates to the Toronto Hilton for midnight rendezvous. Consequently, all carnal aspects of any budding relationship had to be carefully planned. Moreover, when there was a need to satisfy burgeoning lust, Whitney could be as creative as anyone. However, very little money and an amorous female was a major dilemma. The answer: get Bucholz and MacKay to hole up in the closet in the room they shared.

Now, how all this intrigue worked out no one is telling. The participants are far too courteous and would never indulge in the game of kiss and tell, but let it be said that MacKay and Bucholz's fortune on the court was in direct proportion to how much time they spent in the closet. They all were successful, and the team won 5-0. So maybe they should have made the same arrangements in Rome in December, it just may have changed the outcome. There is an obscure moral to this story, but no one involved is talking.

- CHAPTER 24 -

More Davis Cup

In 1961, Whitney was again asked to play Davis Cup. The team beat Ecuador, Mexico, and India and lost to Italy in the Inter-Zone. In the Italian loss, Whitney played astonishing well considering he went five sets with Nicola Pietrangeli who was ranked No. 3 in the world. In the final singles match he lost to Fausto Gardini in five extremely close sets. In doubles, Whitney and Donald Dell lost a close match to Pietrangeli and Orlando Sirola. Granted the U.S. lost the Inter-Zone to Italy, but all the matches were extremely well contested, and could have easily gone the U.S.'s way. In addition, the U.S. team was playing in Rome in front of a bunch of crazy Italians. Who knows what would have happened if the close matches had gone the other way; they might not have made it out of Rome in one piece.

Although Whitney loved to win, winning was not his prime motivation. Whitney loved to play tennis for the sheer love of the game. He loved to entertain and he hated matches to end. As Willie Sutton said, "The only time I feel alive is when I'm robbing a bank." The only time Whitney feels alive is when he is on the tennis court. Why he declined to play Davis Cup following the loss to Italy is conjecture. Whitney maintains that his play was not up to Davis Cup standards. The fact is, he trained for Davis Cup in 1961. He ran, went easy on the booze and cigarettes and went five long grueling sets with the third best player in the world. For reasons known only to Whitney, the Italian episode did not ameliorate the inner demon. He did not garner any strength from knowing that he did his very best. Maybe Whitney, in his heart of hearts, felt that his game was not up to the standards he placed on himself, and it was time to move on – only Whitney knows for sure.

- CHAPTER 25 -

Playing With the Rich and Famous

Tennis players have an affinity for drama; maybe that's why so many sordid stories revolve around tennis pros. The lonely homemaker has an affair with the club pro that happened to be an ex-tour player. Rich socialite travels with ex-touring pro, or prominent investment banker names tennis pro as co-respondent in sleazy divorce action. There is a myriad of story lines where the tennis pro is either murdered or a murderer, a drug dealer, or, my personal favorite, a secret agent for the CIA. Except for the secret agent, the tennis pro is always cast as a double-dealing, opportunistic, two-bit operator. You never hear of a TV or movie drama where the golf pro is the villain. Perry Mason never reveals the golf pro as the culprit. It is always the tennis pro.

When Whitney befriended Charlotte Ford and Mini Cushing, the circumstance should have had the potential for some real drama. Charlotte Ford was Ford Motor Company heir and Mini Cushing was the daughter of Alex Cushing, the founder of Squaw Valley. This budding friendship had all the makings of great theater. In reality, poor Whitney was just a little comic relief for a couple of debutantes. Mini and Charlotte may have been genuinely nice people, but at that age they were in it for the fun.

Whitney was invited to several cocktail parties held at Mini's guesthouse in Newport, Rhode Island. These parties usually required formal wear. The only thing black in Whitney's wardrobe was a pair of Chuck Taylor Converse All Star sneakers, the kind that every male student at San Jose State wore for every occasion. Converse All Stars would look a little out of place at a society cocktail party, so Whitney borrowed a tux and dyed a pair of white bucks black.

Parties are to Whitney as sailboats are to water. But for all the ebullient behavior associated with Whitney and his partying antics (like the time he took all his clothes off and jumped in the pool) he is basically shy.

Girls like Mini and Charlotte are Barracudas when it comes to spotting shyness and exploiting it. It took Mini and Charlotte about a New York minute to figure out that teasing Whitney was about as much fun as one could have clothed. Whitney didn't have a chance. As soon as he walked in the door the girls were all over him. They'd grab his arm and steer him around like a rag doll constantly hugging and kissing what they called, "the sexiest face on the tour." Whitney loved the attention once he overcame his bouts of timidity with copious amounts of champagne.

One evening Charlotte ask Whitney if he could drive her powder blue Mustang to Los Angeles. For Whitney, it was a Godsend. He needed to play in the Pacific Southwest Tennis Tournament and he had been mildly concerned with his shortage of traveling funds. Charlotte's offer came at a perfect time. Newport had been fun, the parties had been exciting, but it was time to get out of town.

Whitney, Charlotte, and Mimi hugged, kissed, and bid a joyous adieu. It had been entertaining, and a little taxing. Mini and Charlotte were fun and very energetic, but they were like eating fine chocolate – too much of a good thing can cause irreparable damage.

Whitney guided the Mustang to the interstate and set the speedometer on 85. Somewhere in Ohio Whitney stopped for gas and a six-pack of beer. While the attendant was filling the tank, an angry looking guy walks up to the car and tells

Whitney that he just caught his wife in bed with his best friend, and what were the chances of a ride out of this crummy state. Whitney opened the passenger door and said, "First six-pack is on you."

Conversation between the two travelers was not stimulating. They didn't have a whole lot to say to one another. Whitney was sympathetic to his traveling companion's dilemma, but it wasn't a topic he cared to deliberate.

The hitchhiker enjoyed NASCAR, as do most Midwesterners. Whitney's penchants are well documented, so bonding was not something they both viewed as a priority. Common ground was obtained when they discovered that they both loved to drive with dark lagers between their legs.

This serious love of dark lager was revisited frequently. From the middle of Ohio to the corner of Hollywood and Vine, every 200 miles they stopped for a six-pack.

Whitney dropped his traveling companion on the corner of Hollywood and Vine. The guy shook Whitney's hand and thanked him for the ride; the last thing Whitney saw in his rearview mirror was the guy's hand in the air waving for a cab.

Young Whitney

L/R Jack Darrah, Cliff Mayne, Whitney, Norm Peterson
Bunch of kids hanging out after the Sac. Juniors

Alameda High Rogues Gallery
Whitney and Norm Peterson far right

Page 54—S.F.Examiner ☆☆☆ Mon., May 20, 1968

RAUL CONTRERAS CONGRATULATES VICTOR WHITNEY REED
After latter won Bay Counties Invitational crown

Whitney, Raul Contreras
Tiburon Tournament 1968
Contreras was a Mexican Davis Cupper

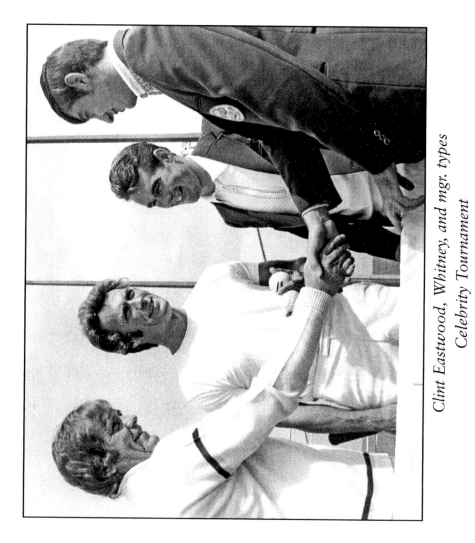

Clint Eastwood, Whitney, and mgr. types Celebrity Tournament

Clint Eastwood, Whitney, Don Hamilton
Carmel Celebrity Tournament

All the best seniors from north and south
Bob Hill organizer at the Vintage in Palm Desert

L/R Eldon Rowe, Pancho Gonzalez, Whitney, Bob Hill

Whitney, Grigry, Olmedo and Emerson
Guy on the left is the botel mgr

Cliff Mayne, Roy Enerson, Whitney, Rod Laver
Claremont Hotel Berkeley Celebrity Gig

L/R Whitney, Dan Rowen, Rick Barry's Partner, Rick Barry
Celebrity Tournament in Lake Tahoe

Ken Rosewall, Yvonne Goolagong, maybe Jane Albert-left with Whitney's cousin Mike Sheridan (Tall guy)

Whitney

Most of the most famous in the sport

Alex Olmedo, J Grigry, Claudia (Blonde) Whitney, Emerson Santa Domingo gig arranged by Grigry

Don Kierbow, Whitney, Bob Hill, Don Gale

*Bob Hill, Whitney
Winning in Portola Valley*

Tom Brown, Whitney, Bob Hill, Eldon Rowe

All the best seniors from north and south again at the Vintage

Bob Hill, Hugh Ditzler, Cliff Mayne, Whitney

Frankie Albert, Bill Cosby, Jack Frost etc

The usual suspects in Santa Domingo
"Meet the Beatles" Whitney ready with the Backgammon case

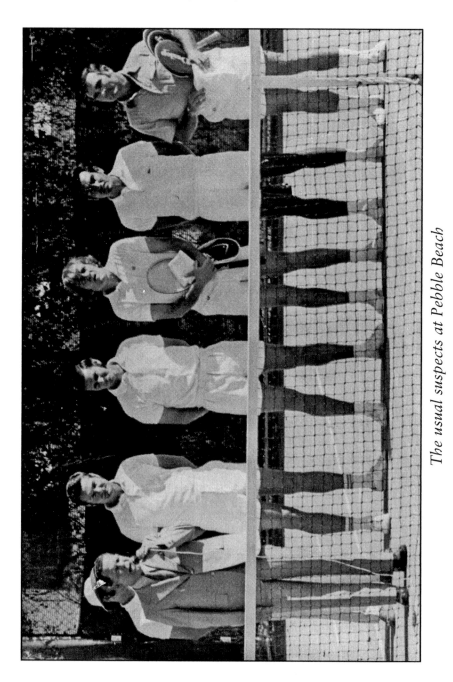

The usual suspects at Pebble Beach

Whitney, Gail Feaster, Jack Frost
In front of Jack's house in Indian Wells

l/r Jackie Cooper, Whitney, Lornie Kuhle, holding court with Rosie Casals

Butch Kerkorian, Don Gale, Whitney Bob Hill
San Jose State circa 1958

Whitney, Jackie Cooper

Jacque Grigry, Whitney
Berkeley Tennis Club Junior Tournament

Don Kierbow, Jack Frost
Jack Kramer called Kierbow the dark horse

The best backhand in the business

Eldon Rowe, Bob Hill, Whitney, Tom Brown

Whitney, Butch Kerkorian, Bob Hill
San Jose State circa 1959

Whitney
Whitney in Palm Springs winning 65's

Eldon Rowe, Pancho, Whitney, Bob Hill

Doug McClure, Jack Frost, Whitney, Yvonne Nopert

Whitney
Some people would starve if it wasn't
for free tournament food

Three highly-rated junior tennis players and a former Davis Cup player paired off in practice doubles at the Pebble Beach Racquet Club last week. The match served as a warm up for the three players now competing in the Western Junior Tennis Tournament at South Bend, Indiana. Pictured above are (Left to Right) Back Row—The Maharajah of Kutch, 1933 Davis Cup player for India; Norman Peterson of Alameda; and John Gardiner, head pro at the Beach Club. Front Row—Jack Frost of Monterey and Whitney Reed of Alameda. In semi-finals play at South Bend yesterday, Frost paired with Hamilton Richardson of Baton Rouge to defeat Ted Rogers and Tim Coss, 6-1, 6-1. Reed and Peterson, top-seeded in doubles play, were eliminated by Bob Perry of Los Angeles and Allen Cleveland of Santa Monica, 4-6, 6-2, 6-2.

Norm Peterson, Jack frost, Whitney, John Gardiner on right
The fellow on the left is the Maharajah of Kutch

Whitney, Claudia

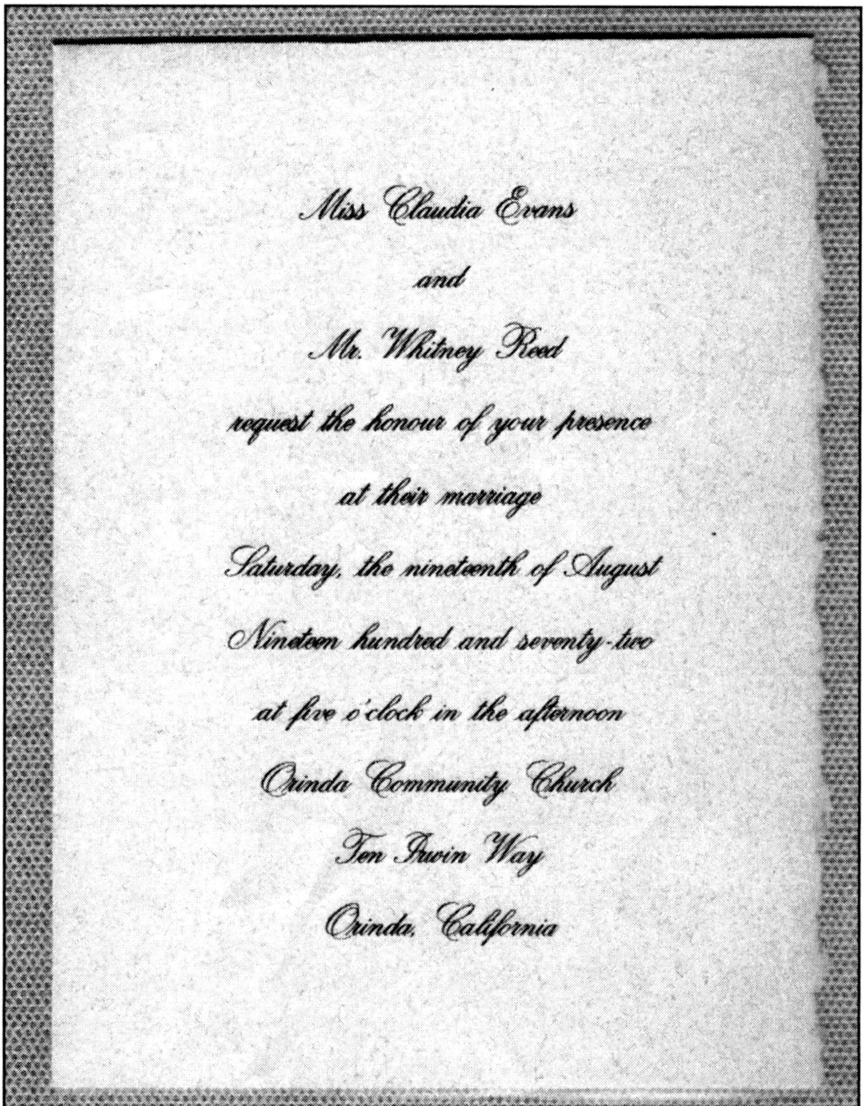

Miss Claudia Evans

and

Mr. Whitney Reed

request the honour of your presence

at their marriage

Saturday, the nineteenth of August

Nineteen hundred and seventy-two

at five o'clock in the afternoon

Orinda Community Church

Ten Irwin Way

Orinda, California

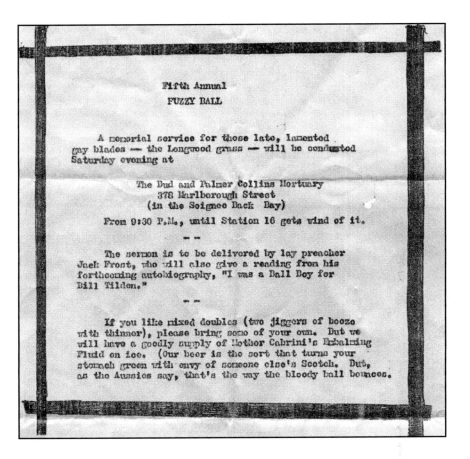

Fifth Annual

FUZZY BALL

A memorial service for those late, lamented
gay blades — the Longwood grass — will be conducted
Saturday evening at

The Dud and Palmer Collins Mortuary
378 Marlborough Street
(in the Soignee Back Bay)

From 9:30 P.M., until Station 16 gets wind of it.

— —

The sermon is to be delivered by lay preacher
Jack Frost, who will also give a reading from his
forthcoming autobiography, "I was a Ball Boy for
Bill Tilden."

— —

If you like mixed doubles (two jiggers of booze
with thinner), please bring some of your own. But we
will have a goodly supply of Mother Cabrini's Embalming
Fluid on ice. (Our beer is the sort that turns your
stomach green with envy of someone else's Scotch. But,
as the Aussies say, that's the way the bloody ball bounces.

Whitney or Pancho's grandmother
According to Pancho, the worst overhead in tennis

Ken Rosewall

Whitney and Jack Frost
Pebble Beach circa 1960

Whitney, Betty Hannis, Yvonne Nopert
Better days for Betty.
Whitney left for Davis Cup and never returned

- CHAPTER 26 -

A Few Chapters Concerning the Women in His Life

Claudia:

Jack Darrah felt that Claudia was the best thing that ever happened to Whitney, and, at some level, Whitney would probably agree. She did a magnificent job in altering his image. Before Claudia, Whitney's reputation did not gain rave reviews. He irritated a few people with his tardiness, and his seemingly irresponsible attitude.

There are numerous instances where he displayed a deep respect and consideration for other people's feelings and possessions. He once returned, completely laundered and folded, a tennis outfit borrowed from Jack Darrah. The fact that this act of consideration occurred two years later did not diminish the effect on Darrah. Pity anyone who dares to cast a disparaging remark in Jack's presence; he or she is in for a full dose of the laundered clothes story.

Whitney's attitudes have always been paradoxical. He has tremendous respect for the game of tennis and its ceremony. If you ask him what is important, he'll say having fun is important. Playing gin with friends is important. Working the crossword puzzle is important. Doing exactly what you want to do, exactly when you want to do it is important. Having a distinct aversion for authority is important. Yet playing Davis Cup is an almost reverential duty. During Davis Cup in 1961, he actually trained for the matches – something as foreign to Whitney as Marlboros and Manhattans are to Denise Richards. Claudia tried to galvanize all these paradoxes into, what she hoped, was Whitney's true character. She felt that the respect he had for Davis Cup and the game of tennis was actually a huge part of Whitney's core values. Thirty years later at his mother's memorial when Whitney announced that he had flunked husbanding on more than one occasion, Claudia shrugged and punched him in the shoulder. For Whiney, the announcement was meant to be clever; for Claudia it was a little more poignant.

When Claudia came along, and this is a wild guess, she saw the uniqueness in Whitney – a uniqueness that tied him to the people who were able to appreciate his uniqueness.

Whitney met Claudia in Reno while he was driving a cab and not, as some have reported, delivering newspapers. His friends lauded the Whitney/Claudia liaison not as a match made in heaven, but as a relief for those who worried about Whitney's socks matching. Now, the fretfulness fell on Claudia. It was no longer Jack Darrah's worry, or Seth Peterson's, or later Dennis Hennessee's.

Claudia was true to the challenge. All of a sudden all Whitney's clothes matched, metaphorically speaking. Entry fees were on time, and he was never late for matches. His hair grew fashionably long and the journalistic comments reported during the Claudia years portrayed him as still the quintessential tennis bum, but a now the tennis bum with style. Even the photographs taken in those years reflect, not the fun-loving tennis player, but a more current rendition of a fun-loving tennis player – probably the long hair and bell-bottom pants helped.

The relationship between Whitney and Claudia is a mystery. A pseudo-psycho babble explanation from me would be irresponsible. Several of Whitney's friends feel that Claudia needed Whitney as much as Whitney needed Claudia. Next time I have lunch with Whitney I'll ask him. He may be in a mood to be candid or he may snort, yawn, and growl.

Claudia promoted the move to Alameda. Marriage may have been the fault of the plebeian attitude of a small town, or marriage may have been Annie's idea. Claudia and Annie were very close friends. Whatever happened or whoever was responsible, marriage was the eventual "kiss of death" for the merger of Claudia and Whitney.

Before marriage, Whitney and Claudia seemed, by all accounts, very happy. They got along famously. When Whitney occasionally drifted afoul of the law from over-imbibing, Claudia would bail him out. If he lost his car returning from an all night gambling session, Claudia would pick him up and bring him home. If Whitney should happen to be involved in an occasional auto wreck, Claudia was there to pick up the pieces. Someone once asked if having a baby would strengthen their relationship, she responded, "One Whitney Reed in this world is enough."

- Chapter 27 -

Legendary Annie Reed

Annie Reed was one tough woman. She was dedicated to her family, friends, and tennis. Although some of her friends would question the friends and tennis in the order of importance.

As a teenager and young adult, Whitney probably thought that the family, friends, and tennis order of importance was a euphemism for stubborn and controlling behavior. Especially when Whitney returned from the Caribbean tour in 1971 (he was 39), Annie wanted to know who his friends were and that Ed Atkinson fellow better not be one of them. Inevitably, when two strong wills collide the fallout was resonant, but in Whitney and Annie's case, the result was ephemeral, never lasting more than the moment.

To Annie, Whitney was her boy and he needed protecting. A task she assumed on August 20, 1932, and from that day in August, she did her very best to care for her boy. Later in life, Whitney returned the favor and did his very best to care for his mom. What more could be asked of a mother or a son?

I wish today that I hadn't suffered the "slings and arrows" of adolescent insecurities when I had the opportunity to get to know Annie and Roland. Unfortunately, she was Whitney Reed's mother, and among Alameda tennis players, Whitney was an unquestioned deity; his name spoken in hushed tones. Too bad, all that celebrity was too much for an average teenage tennis player.

The Reeds played tennis at Washington Park in Alameda almost every weekend for decades. Guys would whisper, "There's Whitney's mom and dad playing on Court 1." We, the local teenage tennis fraternity, avoided playing them like the plague; we didn't want to take a chance on playing poorly. We envisioned Annie telling her son about these dodo teenagers who were no-talents on the tennis court. My contemporaries and I held great notions of some day winning big tournaments partnering with Whitney Reed.

One Saturday morning it happened, we couldn't think of an excuse not to take our turn against the Reeds. When the time came for us to take the court, I was so nervous that four balls went by before I took a swing. Whitney's dad was sure he was playing with a couple of major klutzes, and his mom just looked bored. The Reeds won the set 6-1. We got a game only because my partner came out of a fog to win his serve. We, my partner and I, sat around for about an hour before it was our turn to play again; when the Reeds saw us coming they looked at one another as if to say, watch out here come the klutzes. This time we weren't as nervous and won 7-5. As we walked off the court Annie said, "Quite a difference, nice to see you guys at least figured out which end of the racquet makes contact with the ball." As an adult, the comment was pretty funny, but as a teenager it was devastating.

I continued to avoid the Reeds all summer; it was too risky for a fragile teenaged ego to be exposed to Annie's wit. In the fall, I headed off to college, and pretty much lost track of Annie and Roland.

The first conversation I had with Whitney regarding the possibility of a book, he mentioned that his mom was in good health at 95, and his dad and sister Susan had passed on. I was not surprised that Annie was still with us; even as a teenager I recognized an indomitable sprit.

As we worked on the book, Whitney seemed to get more trusting. We chatted candidly about girls on the tour, who was willing and who was not, who had the best legs and the best personality. He had no problem telling me about guys on the tour who had talent and guys who had no talent. He had no problem in telling me which guys were an easy touch on the poker table, and which guys were good gamblers and tough to beat. From my perspective, we were becoming fairly good friends.

One morning in June, I called Whitney to remind him of our lunch on the following Monday. He said, in his own guttural vocalizations, imitated perfectly by Darrah, that a bed was being delivered for Annie, and he needed to stay home and wait for the delivery. I said to be sure to call me if he needed some help. Whitney said that it was not a problem; he had a friend who was going to help. I mumbled something about helping if his plans ran amok.

Sunday morning Whitney called and said his friend had not called back. I said, "When do you need me?" He said, "One o'clock."

I got to Whitney's at five minutes to 1; he was standing at the door in black warm-up pants and a black Raider sweatshirt. Annie was on a bed in the guest room. Whitney had just given her a shot of morphine; she appeared to me to be already gone. Her mouth was open and her eyes were half closed. The acrid smell of urine was overpowering. Whitney gently touched her face and she moaned softly.

Whitney said the hospice nurse would be by to change her bedding and give her a bath. We went into the dining room and Whitney called to check on the bed delivery. The company delivering the bed said that they had a few stops to make and it would be about an hour.

Whitney and I settled in to wait for the bed and the nurse. We talked about tennis, and perused one of his albums. The album was really cool. He had pictures of every great tennis player from Tony Trabert to Pancho Gonzales. He had a picture of himself taking the net against Ken Rosewall, and one discussing doubles strategy with Clint Eastwood. I almost forgot that Annie maybe taking her last breathe in the other room.

Whitney seemed to have one ear in our conversation and one ear listening for signs of life from his mother's bedroom. Time flew by for the first couple of hours, but about 3 o'clock Whitney started to get anxious. He paced around the room saying, "Where in the Goddamn Hell is that bed." I was worried about the nurse. Pretty soon we would have to change Annie's bedclothes. Whitney knew it and I knew it. About 3:30 the nurse arrived, and I was never so thankful to see anyone in my life. The nurse bathed and changed Annie and got her to eat a little applesauce.

Hospice nurses are no-nonsense people – all business and very proficient. It must take a special person to handle all that death and maintain an air of aloofness. She gave Whitney a few instructions, and before she left she had him administer another dose of morphine. She waited a few moments to make sure she could detect a pulse and then departed, giving Whitney and me a bright smile as she walked out the door. There was no apparent empathy for Whitney's plight or compassion for Whitney's mother's imminent passing. It was just a smile that said you are about to experience something that everyone, if they live long enough, must experience.

It was about 5 o'clock when Whitney started to experience another anxiety attack. The bed had been scheduled for 2 p.m.and now it was well after; he was really getting pissed. We had worked two New York Times crossword puzzles, and exhausted all the tennis gossip imaginable. He got up and paced the room, periodically checking on Annie. Finally, he marched into the backyard for a smoke. I didn't follow him, but I could smell the acrid sent of Camel shorts drifting in from the yard.

I suggested a trip to Taco Bell for some food. Whitney lives close to Webster Street in Alameda; there's a Taco Bell on the corner of Webster and Buena Vista. We drove over in my car, picked up a couple of burritos and raced back to his house. Annie was on her back, mouth open and no sign that she was still with us. Whitney gently stroked her hand. She moved her legs, and he covered her with a sheet.

I'm not sure what we did for the next three hours. We ate our burritos, and I think we worked another crossword puzzle. About 7 o'clock the bed finally arrived. We had planned to have the driver assemble the bed next to Annie's bed and move her over by using the bottom sheet as a sling. The driver had another idea; he wanted to set the bed up in the living room. Whitney wanted no part of that plan; he wanted the bed set up in the bedroom. A minor conflict occurred when the driver said he didn't have time. Whitney straightened up to his full 6 feet 1 inch and said, "We have been waiting since 2 p.m., and you well can spare another 10 minutes to do the job right." Whitney didn't look or sound like William Jennings Bryan, but he made his case nonetheless. The driver looked at Annie and back to Whitney, shrugged and began setting up the bed.

The driver took about 20 minutes to set up the bed. The bedroom is very small; consequently the new bed and the bed Annie was sleeping in filled most of the room. Whitney and I surveyed the room; there were only inches on either side of the two beds. I crawled over Annie's inert body and wedged myself between the headboard and the wall. Whitney wedged himself between the footboard and the closet. We gently took a hold of the corners of the bottom sheet, and as carefully as possible, moved Annie from one bed to the other. Annie continued to moan softly through out the ordeal. She was so thin; it was like moving a small child.

Once Annie was comfortably settled in the new bed, our next problem was to dismantle the old bed. Roland had assembled the bed 30 years ago. He was a jet mechanic, and the bed was tighter than the rivets on one of the F4s he used to work on. It took us an hour to loosen the bolts so we could even start to disassemble the bed. We had to work over and around Annie, and we were doing everything possible not to disturb her. Watching her lying on the bed while we tried to jockey the pieces of the frame over her motionless body was not an experience I care to revisit. I'm sure Whitney felt the same way. A lot of the tension left his face when finally the bed, Annie, and all the medical equipment were back in place

Death is an equal opportunity employer. It doesn't discriminate. We can be rich or the poor, and all the colors of the rainbow. It may allow us to live a long and meaningful life as in Annie case, or it may take our children or grandchildren before they've had the opportunity to take their first step. Death is a real piece of work, a dispassionate, unemotional piece of crap. But worse, it's menacing and intimidating; it makes life look like a giant unmanageable game – not worth the extra effort it takes to finish strong.

Death practices its vocation ruthlessly. It does its work, and in the process may remove from the individual every shred of dignity and nobility. In Annie's case, death was particularly vicious. It allowed her to linger to a point where she was almost unrecognizable. A wisp of white hair and white flesh, the only outward sign of life, trickles of saliva making a pattern down the side of her mouth.

Annie mercifully died on June 18, 2005.

- CHAPTER 28 -

Ann Haydon-Jones

Whitney was no Lothario. If he wound up with a paramour at the end of an evening, nine times out of 10 he was the one hauled off to some secluded rendezvous. To Whitney, girls seemed to be an enjoyable distraction between performances, not a fulltime pursuit. Some members of the touring fraternity considered a female as an adjunct to the task at hand; that is, almost as important as the trophy at the end of a tournament.

Whitney's interests were a little more subtle and varied. If a woman entered his life, it was at her own peril. He wasn't about flowers, expensive dinners, or moonlight walks. He wasn't about fidelity, and, at his own admission, he flunked husbanding more than once. When Ann Haydon made a cursory and abbreviated appearance in Whitney's life, it was, for Whitney, like looking in a mirror.

Ann Haydon was a super tennis player. In 1967 she should have won Wimbledon, but she lost to Billy Jean King 11-9, 6-4. A leg injury diminished the efficiency of her all-court game. In 1969, on her 14th try, she finally won Wimbledon by beating Billy Jean 3-6, 6-3, 6-2. Along the way, it was necessary to dispatch Nancy Richey and Margaret Court, the fifth and first seeds – not bad for the daughter of a table tennis duo from Birmingham, England.

Ann was 5-foot-7, 135 pounds with a round, delectable figure in the Baywatch tradition. She was a stalwart participant in her country's quest for Wightman and Fed Cup victories, but it was in France that she really excelled, winning the singles in 1961 and '66), reaching the finals in '63, '68 and '69) and winning the doubles in '63, '68 and '69).

Ann met Whitney in Montego Bay, the cruise ship of amateur tennis. The place was what Las Vegas purports to be now

– what happens there, stays there. The Caribbean Tour was where the player could relax, enjoy the sun, and recharge for the coming majors. Allen Fox beats Rod Laver, Rod Laver drinks more beer than Tony Roche, and Whitney winds up cavorting with Ann Haydon.

Whitney feels that he got the best of the deal. Ann was fun. She was easy to be with, and he had an affinity for cute, buxom, shorthaired blonde women. Neither Ann nor Whitney was planning a lasting future siring a gaggle of blond tennis player. It was transitory fun in the sun. They soaked up the Caribbean environment, and then moved on.

Whitney is the most uncomfortable when his social life interferes with tennis. The women who have held his interest for longer than a New York minute have either been tennis types or presented no challenge to his tennis existence. From Whitney's perspective, his liaison with Ann started with a pop and ended with a fizzle. After the Caribbean connection, Ann and Whitney played mixed doubles at Wimbledon. They made it to the third round and lost. Ann was a little more upset then Whitney. In fact, after they picked up their racquets and departed the hallowed grounds of Wimbledon, Whitney never again heard that soft British accent, or felt that equally soft British flesh. It is only a guess, but if Ann and Whitney had won the mixed, we may have seen a bunch of Haydon-Reeds sprinkled around the tennis world. With Whitney's touch and feel for the game and Ann's fierce competitiveness, a Haydon Reed may have eclipsed Sampras as the premier player of our generation.

- CHAPTER 29 -

Joanna

In August of 2005, Whitney decided to make the quest to the desert, but first he needed to stop over in Southern California to visit his ex-wife and son. Whitney Jr. was visiting his mom from New Hampshire for a respite from school and a chance to get some Southern California sunshine. Whitney called me and asked if he could hitch a ride to Pasadena. The plan was to meet up with a friend of Whitney's in downtown in Los Angeles. This friend would then transport him to Palos Verdes Estates. The plan sounded fine to me. I would get a chance to spend seven hours of interrupted conversation with Whitney, and Whitney would get to spend a little time with his son.

At the last minute, the plans were changed. Whitney had an epiphany, he pictured his friend Shanghaiing him to Newport Beach, and forcing him to drink beer and chase poor unsuspecting women. Whitney at 73 is working on a more responsible image, so with a note of sadness, he told his friend thanks, but he needed to be conscientious this time.

When I arrived at Whitney's house, he was ready to go – bright-eyed and bushy-tailed, coffee in one hand and golf clubs in another. What was amazing, it was 4 a.m.

Somewhere around the Modesto turnoff, I asked Whitney how old his friend was. He thought for a second and said 70 or so. I immediately got a mental picture of two 70-plus guys chasing a couple of middle aged women, wearing bikinis, down the Strand in Manhattan Beach. It was not that farfetched. I can't speak for the rest of the world but in Southern California a lot of older women look very good, and the possibility of running into an aging female tennis player, in a bikini, on the Strand, who may remember Whitney Reed, is not that remote.

The ride to the Harris Ranch in Coalinga was a trip. Some of the stories were familiar, and some I can never repeat. He knew I had the recorder on but he went on about one romantic interlude unabashed. If I ever shared the tale, even with my doubles partner Pete Pinto, who is also a close friend, I'd be persona-non-grata in a few well-known tennis clubs, and the book would have an X-rating.

The ride from the Harris Ranch to Joanna's home was almost as much fun as the first half of the trip.

I'm so used to Interstate 5, I know where it's possible to go 100 mph, and I know where all the CHP hide. I gave Whitney fits, and inadvertently scared the crap out of him. He spent half the trip jamming his foot on an imaginary brake, and the other half screaming at me to slow down. I thought it was truly ironic, one of the biggest hellraisers of modern times screaming like a baby because of a little speed.

I had to slow down or I'd waste a great opportunity. He was about to tell me a funny story about Erik Van Dillon playing Bobby Riggs. I had the choice: laugh myself silly watching Whitney squirm, or hear a funny story about Bobby Riggs. I chose Bobby Riggs.

Erik was playing Bobby at the LA Tennis club for fun. Erik was a teenager; Bobby was in his 40s. Bobby was never malicious, according to Jack Kramer, although he would stretch a few points of propriety. During this particular match Erik thought Bobby was cheating. Balls that were within six inches one way or another were called out, or so it seemed to Erik. Erik had to constantly correct the score, Bobby would call 30-all when it was 40-5. Bobby was laughing and Erik was fuming. It was getting comical, and Bobby was loving every minute of it. He was looking up into the stands picking out friends and winking outrageously.

We finally made Santa Monica and the LA traffic, our speed went from 85 mph to 5 mph. Whitney finally relaxed his death grip on the dashboard, and started looking for Joanna's turnoff. A series of off ramps and right turns lead to Pacific Coast Highway and eventually Joanna's apartment. We unloaded travel bags, shoe bags, and tennis bags. Whitney stood alongside the Pilot for a few seconds, took a deep breath, straightened his shoulders and walked across the street to Joanna's front door.

Whitney's relationship with Joanna was tumultuous. Joanna is Italian with a Virginia Wolf demeanor. Whitney is roguish with a Gingerman mentality. They were married for seven years and produced one son: Whitney Reed Jr.

Whitney had met Joanna in Palm Springs in 1983. It was not a typical Whitney Reed "fun in the warm California sun" interlude. His usual MO was a couple of drinks, some natty bar conversation, and a promise to do it all over again at the next tournament; anything more than a frivolous connection was not Whitney. When the final ball flew into the net, or the final lob landed in the corner, or whatever, when game, set, and match was announced, Whitney was out the door.

In Joanna's case the "see you next tournament" turned out to be Salt Lake City and the National Indoors. More parties, slick conversation, and a little hand holding under the Mormon Tabernacle gave rise to a Bakersfield reunion.

Whitney always has a good time playing tennis, and holding hands and playing mixed doubles with Joanna made it even more fun. The reunion at the Rio Bravo Tennis Club was perfect; Whitney's penchant for drifting into the landscape when the finals were over took a unique turn. In fact, at the end of the tournament Whitney faced a grave dilemma: He could "slip out the back Jack" and go merrily north with Dennis Hennessee, or he could "make a new plan Stan" and head south with Joanna.

He headed south.

Twenty-one years later, he's standing in front of Joanna's apartment in Palos Verdes Estates.

I don't know what he was thinking when he hitched up his pants and crossed the street to Joanna's apartment, but the quote "I'd rather be in Philadelphia" comes to mind.

Whitney called two days later asking if I was inclined to take a short trip to LA for lunch with Ed Atkinson. I said, "Great. Ask Ed if he could get Alex Olmedo to come along." Whitney said he'd try.

I was late getting to Joanna's apartment; Whitney was standing on the corner in the same outfit he had on two days before. We raced up the freeway. Jerry's Deli in Beverly Hills was the destination, and the coolest joint in town from a Northern Californian's perspective. There are more attractive people in Beverly Hills than anyplace else on the planet, and on that Thursday, they were all having lunch at Jerry's. We were late and Ed had left, so Whitney and I had lunch and enjoyed the scenery. We found out later that Ed had waited for 30 minutes then went on his way. Too bad, it would have been fun listening to Ed and Whitney reminiscing.

On the trip back to La Quinta, I wanted to get a better feel for Joanna as a person. I knew they were married for seven years, but the chemistry that attracted them to one another was a mystery to me. Joanna was an academic, by all accounts an achiever, and very smart. Whitney is very smart, noncommittal, and enigmatic. Meshing those qualities to form a successful union seems equivalent to Angelina Jolie becoming a successful nun.

I asked Whitney, as we pulled on to Highway 10, what finally precipitated the end of his marriage to Joanna. He did his Whitney impression – short cough, long sigh that sort of sounds like a growl, and a long look at the foothills. After about 10 minutes of foothill-looking he said, "I left her stranded at the LA airport with no money, and obviously no ride home. She had to borrow $20 from a fellow traveler. When I finally got home she said among other things, 'We need a divorce.' "

It's October 27, 2005, I'm having lunch with Joanna next week – her account of the aforementioned scenario should be interesting.

- CHAPTER 30 -

Judy Carnivale

The years went by like rocket fire. Whitney played the part of Whitney, winning against all odds and losing to the fireman from Bakersfield. He and Don Kierbow beat everyone in doubles when they decided to monitor the midnight therapy. In one of the fun-filled years, Whitney actually lost in the finals of 55 singles and won the 45 singles. When you think about it, that is a monumental feat. Senior players are tough; they train, practice and take the tour very seriously. There are a couple of people who actually employ trainers, coaches, and practice partners. Making the transition from one age group to another is thorny, but at 57 winning a national tournament in the 45 age group is extraordinary.

Whitney met Judy in a bar. What was unusual about that occurrence is that Judy doesn't drink. She had just finished playing tennis at Palm Valley Tennis Club in Palm Desert. She and a friend stopped off to have a soft drink and enjoy the ambience, and Palm Valley has a bunch of ambience. The bar on the main level over looks the ninth fairway of the golf course and is one of the prettiest spots in the desert. Whitney was chatting with Dennis when Judy popped up and said, "Me and my friend are going to lunch – you want to come?" Whitney and Dennis suggested the Nonchalant in Palm Desert, and that was the start of a wonderful romance.

So what attracted Judy to one of the great bar hoppers of modern times? I think it was his harmless appearance. He exudes this kind of helplessness that some women find irresistible. (My daughter's observation.)

In some respects, Judy was very good for Whitney, almost as good as Claudia was. I say that because I really like Claudia, and I've never met Judy. However, I've found several postcards and notes to Annie that suggest Judy had Whitney's best interests at heart. One in particular, a postcard from the East Coast that extols Whitney's winning several gold balls, and how well he was taking care of himself. I got the distinct impression that Judy was a caring person and respected Annie's concern for her son.

Whitney was with Judy from January 1991 until they fell out of love in 1998. Judy was married to an apple king from the state of Washington, so it was the kind of situation that always puts a strain on a budding romance. "I can't see you this weekend, my husband's in town" is difficult to deal with on a long-term basis. From Whitney's perspective, it was probable pretty cool – all the fun and little responsibility. Judy would fly in to wherever Whitney was playing and then zip home when the fun was over. She had a seasonal home in the San Diego area that was a perfect getaway for Whitney and her. Dennis Hennessee feels that Judy wanted Whitney to morph into Mr. Responsibility. When she realized that morphing was not in Whitney's vocabulary, for sheer self-preservation she decided to move on.

Whitney, at times, suggests that Judy is the one that got away. That may be true, or it may be that he was experiencing a sense of his own mortality. Whitney had turned 60 when they met; guys turning 60 sometimes feel the Grim Reaper at their door, and that can be kind of scary. Whitney may have felt that this was his last chance for happiness. After admittedly flunking husbanding, this was a chance for redemption. The problem was, Judy already had a husband, a husband with a lot of money, and all Whitney had was charm and incredible talent on a tennis court.

When it comes to women, Whitney and about a zillion other men in the universe follow the line of least resistance. Show us a pretty face, a pair of long legs, and we're captivated. If, in addition, that pretty face has a modicum of personality, a touch of class, and a penchant for a warm bed we're doomed.

Poor men run around clueless, we think that this great deal is never going to end; all we need to do is show up with a bouquet of flowers, a silly grin, and life, love, and the universe are ours. Unfortunately, for Whitney and the rest of us poor souls, it doesn't quite work that way.

Women are always concerned with reality. When they sense a lack of commitment, they immediately go into attack mode. They start thinking in terms of: One, this guy plays great tennis, he's OK in the sack, he knows which fork to use, but can he support me in the fashion to which I've become accustomed? Two, will I find someone else who is a better tennis player, is better in the sack, and who can support me in a better fashion? All this womanly reality is tough on us; we hear words like commitment, responsibility, and direction and a lot of us feel that it's time to either "slip out the back, Jack," or start selling shoes and shopping for baby clothes. Whitney was too old for baby clothes, and too contented with his life in tennis shorts to change professions.

Judy may have decided that life in Washington was not so bad after all. She may have wearied of her perception of Whitney's lack of direction and commitment. Whatever it was, the relationship waned and finally died in 1998.

- CHAPTER 31 -

Flunking Husbanding – Flunking Relationshiping

The Last Word Where Women are Concerned

Whitney flunked husbanding, because there is no room in his life for anyone but Whitney. He is totally self-absorbed; yet all the women in his life seem to have a genuine affection for him. Claudia flew out from Houston when his mother passed away and literally took control of everything. She organized his affairs, planned the memorial, and put in motion the remodeling of the Alameda property. Whitney could have bumbled through and everything would have probably worked out, but Claudia made it very easy.

At the memorial, when Whitney announced to the group of family and friends that he was a horrible husband, Claudia laughed and punched him on the shoulder.

Judy Carnivalle called when Whitney's mom passed away. The call may have been pure chance, but it gave Whitney some closure (not my favorite expression). They chatted for a while reminiscing.

- CHAPTER 32 -

Who Said Tragedy?
or
A Funny Thing Happened
On the Way to Winbleton

In 1960, a year before Whitney was ranked No. 1 in the United States, he made it to the third round at Wimbledon. Playing Wimbledon is a heady experience for anyone; playing Neal Fraser in the third round on Centre Court is mind-numbing terror for most players. For Whitney it was a chance to perform on the most prestigious piece of tennis real estate in the world.

Neale Fraser was a great player; he was ranked No. 1 in the world in 1959. In 1960 he was again ranked No. 1 and in the process he won both Wimbledon and Forest Hills. He was a great volleyer and possessed a wicked left-handed kick serve. He and Whitney had done some serious carousing in Montego Bay. In fact, Neale thinks he lost to Whitney a couple of times in the Caribbean, but he's not sure.

Playing Wimbledon, if you were from the colonies, definitely required some schooling in protocol from the officials. These fellows, with a proper public school inflection, instructed players on proper deportment, how to address the Royal box, where to stand, and, for the women, how to curtsy. Actually, every player received the same instruction; it was only fair to the players, and Wimbledon was scary enough without adding a dose of humiliation to the mix.

Whitney endured the counseling with good humor, because it was not a social faux pas that concerned him. When most players were thinking, "Please God, I don't need to win, but I'd sure appreciate it if you could keep me from looking like an ass," Whitney was wondering about wine, women, and song.

Just when he thought he was about to spend the evening before the Fraser match in some sleazy pub playing darts for shillings, he ran into an old Air Force buddy. The Air Force buddy said he had a hot poker game set up with some locals. Whitney, having never met a card game he didn't love, almost sprained an ankle getting out of his hotel room.

The game was everything the Air Force buddy had purported it to be: lots of money and players with moderate skill. The problem was not distancing the players from their wallets; it was getting the never-ending poker game to end. The sun was just breaking over Westminster before Whitney could extricate himself and get back to the hotel and his bed. He left a 12 p.m. wake up call and settled in for some much needed rest.

Either the hotel made a mistake or Whitney slept through the call, but the first thing Whitney noticed when he opened one red eye was the clock clicking on 1:30 p.m. He flew out of bed, ran an electric razor over his face, and was out the door in 10 minutes flat.

A Wimbledon tradition is to play the featured match on center court at 2 p.m. sharp. That gave Whitney 20 minutes to get to Wimbledon, listen to the protocol official, and be on the court. A cinch. He jumped in a cab, waved some pounds in the driver's face and yelled, "Get me to the church on time."

He sat back in the seat and suddenly felt the beginning of a panic attack. He had left his racquets in the back of his Air Force buddy's car. This was a first even for Whitney. He was driving down a London suburb road at 40 mph-plus, on his way to play Centre Court Wimbledon with no racquet.

The cab pulled up in front of the club with about a minute to make it to Centre Court. He jumped out of the cab and ran through a gaggle of spectators and into the men's locker room. He grabbed a passing ball boy and pleaded with him to borrow a racquet. The shocked ball boy handed Whitney a new

Jack Kramer and, in true English fashion, wished him "Jolly good luck."

Whitney ran right by the startled protocol person and onto Centre Court.

Fraser's personality was as unflappable as Whitney's. Although older, he was Australian in the Newcombe tradition. Consequently, he may have thought it a hoot to see a smiling Whitney, borrowed racquet in hand, standing next to him on the most hallowed ground in tennis.

Fraser reached out and took a hold of Whitney's elbow and whispered, "You need to acknowledge the Royal Box."

After 10 seconds of terror, Whitney straightened his shoulders and bowed in a most humble fashion. The problem was the Royal Box faced east and Whitney's offering also was directed east, thus giving the Royal Box an unobstructed view of his posterior.

The stadium went very quiet. Fortunately, Fraser was in the moment; he reached out and casually took Whitney's arm and turned him around. Whitney, in one motion, whirled around, supported by Fraser's hand, and bowed most humbly.

Whitney's first thought was, "Oh shit!" His second thought was, "Why didn't I listen more carefully to the protocol guy." His third and final thought was, "They're never going to ask me back, even if I become No. 1 in the world."

Whitney has told the Wimbledon story dozens of times in every banquet, pool hall, and bar on the planet. It's one of those few stories in sports that can't be corrupted. It is so simple, an athlete with a fun-loving, iconoclastic reputation makes the ultimate innocent peccadillo. The question is what was the reaction in the Royal Box? A safe guess would be that the Duchess of Kent has shared the story a few times, maybe at a tea or reception, certainly not in front of the same audience as Whitney's. It's difficult to imagine the Duchess sitting in a bar in Alameda relating a story of a tennis player, playing in the third round of Wimbledon, showing her his clothed posterior..

So Where's The Tragedy?

Defining tragedy in life is a convoluted task. Considering Whitney's outwardly devil-may-care approach to life, the task is monumental. If you ask him what the most tragic experience of his life was, he would growl, clear his throat, and say, "Beats me." There would be a short intermission, a period of dead air, he would look off contemplatively, and I think he would say the Davis Cup match against Pietrangeli.

The intersectional match was played in Rome; Whitney was leading two sets to one and was up 4-2 in the fourth at 30-40 with Pietrangeli serving. Then came the pickle; the match was postponed due to darkness. Not only postponed, but postponed after the worst call in Davis Cup history. The Italian linesman called a ball good that was clearly three or four inches out. Whitney was heading for the sidelines assuming all he had to do was hold serve for a trip to Australia when he heard "bella, bella." Whitney spun around and started for the Italian linesman. Dave Freed, the U.S. captain, thought Whitney was going to throttle the little Italian. He darted on the court and grabbed Whitney from behind.

Whitney was flabbergasted; he was being grabbed by Freed, the Italian crowd was going crazy, and he was looking at Pietrangeli's ball mark that was a good four inches past the baseline. He didn't consider beating the living shit out of the linesman until later. Now, all Whitney could think was, "Son of a bitch, there goes our trip to Australia."

Dave Freed was, by all accounts, not receptive to Whitney's oblique lifestyle. Freed didn't understand that Whitney needed to unwind after a fiery couple of hours on the tennis the court. Freed was the original "eat a steak, get eight hours of sleep and everything will be fine" type of coach. He didn't understand that midnight marauding for Whitney was necessary for him to maintain his equilibrium. When he suggested that Whitney hit the rack at a reasonable hour, he might as well have told the Italian captain to start packing for Australia.

The loss to Pietrangeli was doubly disappointing because of the courageous effort of Jon Douglas, who, with about one-half the talent of Whitney, fought valiantly and defeated a much more accomplished player in Fausto Gardini. Whitney never blamed anyone for the loss, not Dave Freed, not the Italian linesman who made the worst call in the history of the Davis Cup, and not the raucous Italian crowd. In Whitney's mind, he should have beaten that "friggin' Italian" in straight sets.

In every bar in the world, someone is invariably looking into his or her beer and thinking, "I could have been a contender." At every cocktail party on the planet, some bore is preaching as to what might have been.

Not Whitney, he experienced true vindication.

Twenty years later Whitney is sitting in the Player's Pub at Wimbledon enjoying a beer with Lew Hoad. A skinny little Italian taps Whitney on the shoulder and says, "Remember me; I was the linesman in Rome."

Pietrangeli was Whitney's tragedy. Our tragedy is that we will never see a Whitney Reed type in big-time tennis, and that's sad. We will never see a player move about the playing surface and half-volley winners from any spot on the court. No one lobs off of the volley anymore, and that was Whitney's signature shot. Players today occasionally hit the ball between their legs while running away from the net; Whitney hit the ball between his legs while running toward the net.

Never again will we see a player insist on playing in a rainstorm because it was pure and healthful, and the benefit derived from exposure to such purity far outweighed the danger of playing on slippery footing. Whitney and Jack Frost did just that at the National Doubles at Longwood in 1973. Whitney called it "swinging in the rain." Today the sponsors, the USTA officials, and the mothers of the players would have called out the National Guard and ordered the everyone off the court at gunpoint. No one in their right mind would risk millions in prize money for a little innocent fun.

The tragedy for those who truly love the game is that there are no Whitney Reeds on the horizon. There is too much money at stake. Today if a player shows promise, he or she ends up at the Bollettieri Academy in Florida with the best facilities known to man. Trainers, coaches, nutritionists, and sport psychologists cater to the players' every need. There is little room for a fun- loving, irreverent, insouciant, type of player. Nick Bollettieri puts out tennis players; from his perspective, if you want to entertain, join the circus.

I wonder what would have happened if Annie had taken a young Whitney to the Bollettieri Academy? People who know Whitney will say that Whitney would have not have been successful in a Bollettieri atmosphere – too many rules and too structured. They say that his creativity may have never surfaced, and his quirky personality would have been lost forever. My guess is that there would be fewer virgins on the women's tour.

Whitney did not give a hoot for propriety; he was just out to have a good time, and a good time was playing tennis, anyplace, anywhere, anytime. If sports are the embodiment of life, then Whitney's tragedy is that he was pretty close to the best in one area and an abject failure in another. That's not a bad thing; how many of us would trade our souls to be the best in our chosen endeavor, even if it meant being the worst in every other pursuit? I know many people who would walk up to the devil and hand him their soul if it would assure a win at Wimbledon.

Whitney scrambled uninhibitedly to the top of the tennis world. As Don Budge said, "Whitney would get the ball back no matter what: kick it, bat it, scoot it, or push it – in Whitney's mind the ball was going back." When he woke up one morning and realized that he was the No. 1 player in the United States, he figured that the No. 1 player should have strokes like Jack Kramer. That was a mistake. Whitney was a great player when Whitney played Whitney; Whitney playing Jack Kramer didn't work. When his ranking started to drop like a bad habit, Whitney sat around with a beer in his hand wondering, "Why me, Lord." Finally, Pancho Gonzalez whacked him along side the head and reminded him of a few salient facts, like "You're Whitney Reed, dip shit, start playing like him." Thanks to Pancho, Whitney avoided the tragedy of failure, and started emulating Whitney Reed. He experienced an epiphany: You don't need Jack Kramer strokes to win; Whitney Reed strokes are just fine.

Mickey Mantle said, "If I had known I would live this long I would have taken better care of myself." Whitney said, "If I had known I would live this long I would have tried harder to have more fun." Mickey's comment occurred after he was diagnosed with a serious liver disease; it was viewed by the public as thoughtful and introspective. Fortunately, Whitney's quote occurred in his living room, and was heard by his girlfriend and me. I thought it was dorky and his girlfriend thought it was funny. Sports Illustrated would have called it tragic and an abuse of a fine talent.

Whitney's life is paradoxical. Born in 1932, Whitney just missed the lost generation, and he was in the Air Force during the Beat generation. Maybe he got the best of both generations? As a spirit between generations, he could claim the influences of Dos Pasos, Stein, and Henry Miller, as well as Ginsburg, Kerouak, and Ferlingetti. Maybe Whitney is a tragic soul lost between generations – an enigma stuck between Miller and Ginsburg. Actually, if it was Whitney's choice, he would prefer being lost between Miller and Budweiser.

He and Jack Frost playing "swinging in the rain" is a youthful example of social disruption – thumbing your nose at propriety. A more viable case in point was the use of his talent. He needed to prove that he could win his way. Swinging volleys, drop shots from the baseline, all the shots that tennis pros abhor. The problem with being your own man is that it can lead to a ton of heartbreak. As corny as it sounds, no man is an island; no man can fight City Hall. Whitney didn't fight City Hall, he simply ignored it, and in his 75th year on the planet he is still ignoring it.

Maybe Whitney feels that if you ignore reality, reality can't hurt you. Maybe that's why some folks feel Whitney is aloof and not always in the present. If he feels threatened, he withdraws, giving the appearance of being remote. Even the latest article in the Oakland Tribune mentions his faraway gaze. Next time around, he may take reality head-on, no growling, no wit, and no clever retorts – just straight from the shoulder gut-wrenching living. Now that would be our tragedy.

In discussing the tragedies in Whitney's life, it is beyond me to judge the effect of the death of his mother, father, and sister. Whitney is such a private person that I feel that it is impossible for him to articulate his feelings to anyone. Besides, I don't know anyone who would want to start life anew, especially Whitney. What if he was reborn a 3.5?

So at lunch the other day, I asked him straight out: "Excluding your family, your flunking husbanding, and the loss to Larry Nagler in the NCAA finals, what do you feel is your greatest tragedy? It's the loss to Pietrangeli – right?"

- CHAPTER 33 -

What's Tragic For Me — May Not Be Tragic For You

Winning at any cost is a challenging concept. Our society doesn't take losing lightly. We don't say, "Wow! What a great effort, if that last forehand had been a quarter of an inch higher, Spadea as in Arcadia, would have won Wimbledon." We say, "Too bad for that poor shmuck; he just lost a zillion dollars."

We require our athletes to go out and win. When they don't win, they're criticized for lack of effort or lack of talent. When they do win, they're praised for a spirited and tenacious performance. If you equate lack of effort and lack of talent with something bad, and a spirited and tenacious performance with something good, it doesn't take much of a logician to tell the good guys from the bad guys. All you need to do is look at the box scores.

What tremendous pressure it places on the athlete. If I play my heart out and lose, I'm bad. If I run down a cross-court forehand and return it for a winner, I'm good. If I just miss it by a millimeter, I'm bad. No wonder some athletes are always in a state of crisis, their identity changes from one second to another. From the outside looking in, it seems to require the maturity of Christ just to stay balanced. I sometimes feel Ron Artest was justified in beating the daylights out of an idiot fan.

How does all this banal bantering relate to Whitney? We are only talking sports here, folks. And in sport everyone possesses a critic's license. Therefore, in exercising my observations in the territory of my license, I'm saying that part of this opus (Bud Collin's description) is designed to dissuade a few of Whitney's critics, and make a derisory attempt to explain Whitney's behavior – a behavior that some say borders on the irresponsible.

Whitney is a tremendous competitor. In his heyday, he was the best player in the United States, and probably one of the

10 best players in the world. He has played with and beaten the biggest legends in tennis. How he chooses to deal with success and failure is his business. If he pisses off a share of his associates by his approach to life, those associates shouldn't seek his company.

My mother was fond of saying: "The only person you're hurting is yourself." I am assuming she meant that as long as I'm not hurting anyone, my behavior is my business. If Whitney chooses to drink himself silly, smoke two packs a day, and squander his talent, it's his decision. If you choose to play doubles with him, and he shows up late and not in the best of shape, that's your fault. Whitney has a method of dealing with matters that works for him. It may not be conventional or universally accepted, but for all the late nights and over-indulging, he's still sane, standing, and sentient.

Whitney's behavior is more than paradoxical. If he trained, got plenty of sleep, and went easy on the booze, he lost. If he could hang out in some sleazy bar, play shuffleboard, and schmooze with the locals, he won. On the Caribbean Tour, he talked Rod Laver into a late-night tour of the clubs, and the next day Whitney beat a blurry-eyed Laver in straight sets. Whitney told the media afterward that it was no big deal, Laver needed to learn to hit the middle ball.

Bottom line: Whitney was not pathological about winning or losing. He didn't fear losing, and he didn't need losing to feel alive. If he won, it was cool, but he didn't feel that a win was a time for champagne and strawberries. For Whitney, winning was important, but not as important as global warming or world peace, and losing was a drag but not as much of a drag as the starving children on the UNICEF posters. What Whitney could not tolerate and what made him feel like a real bag of crap, was a performance that was not pleasing to watch.

"Just win baby" implies big-time tragedy if you lose. I can't fathom Al Davis embracing a mantra like "Just perform, baby." Yet, if Whitney passes on before I do, you can bet "Just perform, baby" will be on his headstone.

Long Day's Journey at Forest Hills

The tragic for me, tragic for you conundrum has a perfect case in point -- Forest Hills 1961.

There are a few tennis aficionados who feel very strongly that the third round in the 1961 U.S. Championships was the finest contested match in the history of the tournament. Whitney went head-to-head with a player who was destined to become the No. 1 player in the world --- Rafael Osuna.

Rafael Osuna could run the 40 in about 3 seconds flat, or so it seemed. He could stop on a dime and be going a full speed in the other direction before you could blink. If you tried to pass him, he'd simply run down your passing shot. If you tried to rally with him, he'd stand at the baseline and out-duel the devil. He was U.S. Champion in 1963, and twice won Wimbledon doubles. He was ranked No.1 in the world in by the ITF in 1963. He died tragically in an airplane crash on June 6, 1969.

Rafael's electrifying match with Whitney lasted an eternity. The number of great shots could fill half of a Bud Collins epic. Every ball hit would have been an ESPN highlight had ESPN been in existence in 1961.

Neither player gave an inch, Whitney would charge into no-man's-land, angle off half-volleys and lob when Osuna attacked the net. Osuna would chase down drop shots and touch the ball back at angles that defied logic.

When the referee said game, set, and match, both players looked bewildered. Osuna reacted first; he jumped over the net and embraced Whitney. Whitney mumbled something in Whitney language and both players picked up their bags and wandered, totally drained, toward the locker room.

When questioned by a reporter in the locker room, Osuna said that at the moment the referee declared the match over, neither he or Whitney could figure out who won.

The last time Whitney saw Osuna was at San Francisco International Airport. Osuna was on his way to Europe and Whitney was parking cars for Hertz. There was no irony or tragedy to the encounter because Whitney never gave a damn. He may have felt a twinge of embarrassment, but, the fact was, he performed his best against the best in the world on one of tennis's premier stages.

- CHAPTER 34 -

If I'm That Good, The Only Person I'm Interested In Talking To Is God

Some of this rhetoric is leading to another perplexing question: Should we treat extraordinarily talented individuals with a different set of rules? Jack Frost says extraordinary athletes are treated differently from birth. As soon as any child shows exceptional dexterity, strength, and coordination, parents start thinking "Bonus Baby – My kid is going to have a Roger Clemens fastball." In Little League, at the peewee level, when a kid shows speed and unique hand-eye coordination, he or she is treated differently.

In Jack Frost's·case, he says the idea of seeing your name in the sports section and catching the eye of the cute girls was intoxicating. He enjoyed being on stage, on center court. He liked being pulled out of class at 12 years old to play tennis at Pebble Beach Tennis Club. When he got in fights with the tough Sicilian kids in Monterey, it was fun and a challenge, but no one pulled him out of class to fight on the playground. His win-loss record of fights with Sicilian kids did not make the sports section. The cute girls did not root for him to bloody some kid's nose; they rooted for him to beat some kid with a big serve and volley. Jack is a smart fellow, it took him a New York minute to figure out how his bread was buttered.

Jack was treated differently because of his extraordinary athletic ability. He realized at a very young age that he had a talent that set him apart from his peers. He used his talent to do exactly what he wanted to do. He got a scholarship to Stanford, he traveled extensively, he enjoyed the company of some unique people, and he got a Fulbright Scholarship, a doctorate, and a very charming and beautiful wife.

In some respects, Whitney's approach to life mirrored Jack's: He used his extraordinary athletic ability to accomplish exactly what he wanted. In Whitney's case, it was the opportunity to live life by his rules – no 9-to-5 job, no boss, no lunch boxes, and no structure. Art Larsen said it as succinctly as anyone; "I can sell shoes when I'm 50." Whitney said, "Let someone else sell the shoes, I'll play tennis until I'm 90."

Maybe the answer to the question of extraordinary people being treated in an extraordinary fashion is not how we treat them, but how they treat themselves. Jack and Whitney used their talents to satisfy their individual needs. Jack pursued the goals that his environment and background dictated. Whitney did exactly the same thing. He pursued performing on the tennis court, and he did it his whole life. After the glamour of Wimbledon and Forest Hills, he continued to perform from age group to age group. Tennis was and is his life.

Whitney is unique; he'll play anyplace, anytime, and with anyone. One-half the tennis players in Marin County have played with Whitney one time or another; the other half will tell you that they beat him one time or another. All of them will tell you that they had a ball – even the liars.

Jack and Whitney are very unpretentious. They will hug, kiss, dance or chat with everyone. A question, expressing a thought, or merely a blatant statement will sustain a conversation all night. If you go out socially with either Jack or Whitney, the occasion will be fulfilling. If you spend time with Jack and his wife Helenka, the conversation will be erudite, fun, and congenial. He knows all the cool places in the Coachella Valley, and he's on a first-name basis with every chef, waitress, and restaurant owner from Palm Springs to the Salton Sea.

If you spend time with Whitney, the conversation will be equally enjoyable. The difference is you need to listen a little closer to Whitney. His wit is unconventional unless you're a resident of the planet Mars. He can craft the most bizarre comments and make them sound as if they were articulated by Noel Coward.

A social occasion with Whitney is earthy; a social occasion with the Frosts is urbane. Jack and Helenka will suggest a quaint French patisserie with great chocolate torts. Whitney will suggest a smoke-soaked bar with a beat-up shuffleboard. In either case, if you step out with Whitney or the Frosts the interlude will be very enjoyable but consider this a warning – both sojourns are loaded with undeniable risks. With Whitney, it's secondhand smoke and maybe the possibility of being whacked by a pool cue. With the Frosts, the only real danger is the sin of gluttony or the chance of a cardiovascular accident from infusing your arteries with cholesterol.

Jack and Whitney are examples of extraordinary people who used their gifts without the accompanying abuse. They were accessible, unpretentious, and gracious. Their circle of friends is sprinkled with the rich and famous, but they never succumbed to the trappings of celebrity. They had goals that were diametrically opposite, but the avenue to realizing those goals was the same.

I can honestly say that if I had extraordinary talent – extraordinary, in that if I could do something that maybe only a handful of people in the world could do – I would be insufferable. I would make the most selfish basketball player on the planet seem like the reincarnation of Gandhi. In fact, I would only talk to Gandhi. If he wasn't available, I'd only talk to Henry Cabot Lodge.

I am in awe of people who treat their extraordinary talent with cavalier complacency, because I am absolutely certain that I would not.

- CHAPTER 35 -

Whitney said, "I'm No Saint for Christ's Sake."
or
A Tale of Two Renditions

The First Rendition is Hearsay, Folklore.

The Subsequent Rendition is From the Horse's Mouth.

Whitney attracts contention. Consequently, garnering the truth and filtering out the comedy is a not an easy task. Unless one possesses the analytical mind of Jack Frost, or the organized mind of Jim Nelson, sifting truth from fact is a challenge. The problem is, everyone has a Whitney story, and when it is retold a 1000 times, the final rendition often bears little resemblance to the truth.

I am the most flagrant violator of the truth, and I fight it every day. It is so easy to edit and enhance a story about Whitney; he is like fly paper in the way he attracts humor. All he needs is a tiny venue, one person to listen, and folklore is fashioned. Consequently, illuminating the truth and doing justice to his life is a convoluted task.

The folklore

Whitney was sitting in his office at the Harbor Bay Tennis Club when one of the members came strolling along with a proposition. Bill Cosby was playing at Harrah's, and if Whitney would drive to the lake, this member would pay for the gas and give Whitney a $100 for his time. Whitney, never one to pass on a quick $100, fell over his desk trying to get the car keys out of his pocket.

The drive up Interstate 80 was uneventful. They stopped for gas and had a quick lunch, the member paying unceremoniously. Whitney felt a little relieved when the check came and the member reached for it immediately. He knew this member only casually, and you never know what's in store until you get on the open road.

They pulled into the parking lot of Harrah's about mid-afternoon. Whitney had a beer between his legs and a full bladder. He and the member jumped out of the car and ran for the men's room. At Harrah's, the men's room is about two miles from the front entry. They made it, but it was close.

The member handed Whitney a $100 bill and scampered off to the crap tables. Whitney looked at the $100 for about a nanosecond then turned and wandered over to the nearest blackjack table.

The dealer was a cross between Ashley Judd and Wynona Ryder, and it was very hard to concentrate. He'd look up from his cards into a pair of soft brown eyes and was oblivious to the fact that face cards count for 10. The Ashley Judd/Wynona Ryder dealer was remarkably cold, and before the pit boss could make a change he was a few hundred ahead. Whitney was mildly surprised when the dealer smiled, tapped a $20 chip on the table, and walked away. Surprised in that he had a couple of stacks of $20 chips in front of him, and surprised that he was so enamored with the dealer that he hadn't noticed flipping her the $20 chip.

Whitney sat back on his stool and waited for the arrival of the next dealer. He sipped his drink and noticed, over the brim of his highball glass, that the member was banging his head on the rail of the crap table. This was bad. Gamblers shrug their shoulder when they lose a little. Walk away, thinking tomorrow is another day, when they lose a lot. When gamblers bang their heads on the rail of a crap table, it is usually not a good sign.

The member stopped when a worried pit boss tapped him on the shoulder and reminded the member that banging your head on a crap table was unacceptable casino behavior.

Whitney's heart rate jumped about 30 percent; neither Harrah's nor its counterpart across the street, Harvey's, was a place where any misbehavior was tolerated. In the 1960s and '70s the casinos on the South Shore of Lake Tahoe were small enclaves, they made the rules and vigorously enforced them. If you bent, bowed, or tried to usurp any of Harrah's or Harvey's conventions, the chances of ending up in a dumpster were pretty good. Whitney could almost visualize the headlines in the Alameda Times Star: "Local tennis pro and former Davis Cup player watches as prominent Alamedan is bashed silly by casino ruffians in Tahoe gambling establishment."

Whitney made a decision; either the member would assure the pit boss that his behavior was a momentary act of diminished capacity or Whitney would fetch the poor bastard from the local infirmary. He barely knew this guy, and he knew from past experience that if he tried to intervene he would wind up sharing the dumpster.

Fortunately, cooler heads prevailed. The pit boss must have thought it mildly amusing, because the next thing Whitney experienced was the pit boss, with his arm around the member, laughing uproariously. Whitney found out later what was so funny: The member tried to talk the pit boss into backing him in a gaming scheme. The Harrah's employee must have figured that the member was either deranged or joking. He must have felt that no sane person would even consider such a proposal.

Two minutes later, the pit boss is walking away shaking his head, and the member is heading in Whitney's direction. The member walked up to Whitney, looked down at all the chips and asked to borrow a couple of hundred.

Whitney is the most tolerant person on the planet. He plays tennis with me whenever I ask. He plays tennis with his girlfriend whenever she asks. If I called him up and said, "I'll pick you up in 10 minutes; we are going to watch grass grow." He'd say, "Sure let me get a coat." If I asked to borrow his Wimbledon jacket, he'd say, "Sure, it's in the closet." Consequently, when the member asked to borrow a few hundred, Whitney simply waved at his chips.

Whitney sat at the blackjack table through another run of luck and two more visits by the member, the last being worth $500. Not even Jimmy the Greek could continue to win at a pace that could underwrite the member's losing streak. Just about midnight, the member borrowed back the original $100.

Whitney got up from the blackjack table and made a call to Bill Cosby. (How it got through to Cosby is a mystery) As the story goes, Cosby gave Whitney a little crap, then "comped" them a room.

How they got off the mountain remains a mystery today. Whitney says they must have coasted all the way back to Alameda.

The Truth From the Horse's Mouth

Whitney played tennis with a lot of celebrities, because he was enjoyable to be around. He didn't whack a serve so hard that it seemed to disappear; that was Rick Barry's trick. He didn't look or act like a world class athlete. He'd keep the ball in play so everyone had a chance to run down a short ball or he'd throw up a lob that even my grandson could hit.

Dan Rowan, Clint Eastwood, and Bill Cosby were occasional doubles partners. Now and then one of them would call Whitney to play doubles, and that was fine with Whitney. He'd jump in what ever transportation was available and head for Carmel if it was a Eastwood's gig, or Los Angeles if it was a Cosby affair. I think he was more interested in the venue than the participants. A celebrity tournament meant good booze, attractive women, and performing in wonderful arenas. Rubbing elbows with a bunch of movie stars held no real fascination for Whitney, unless those elbows were attached to Angelina Jolie. With the exception of Ms. Jolie, Whitney, if the crowd was large enough, would have been happy playing in South Central LA or Beverly Hills; it didn't matter.

Whitney didn't discriminate. He'd play doubles with Pete Pinto or Pancho Gonzalez. He'd play with Pete because they both look like aging villains in a B movie (even the handsomest of fellows wear with age) or he'd play with Pancho because he was one of the players that Whitney truly admired. From Whitney's perspective, he was not selfish with his talent; he would loan it to anyone, and all you needed to do was ask.

This indiscriminate giving of oneself is admirable, but it comes with a burden. As my dad used to say, "There are givers and takers in this world and never for a moment believe that a good deed will go unpunished." He was also fond of saying, "There is no such thing as a free lunch."

If I give you something, dear, should I expect anything in return? Whitney never expected anything from anyone; he gave of his talent indiscriminately, although he did get into a situation in Tahoe that required him to ask a favor of a celebrity friend.

Whitney was sitting in the bar at the Harbor Bay Tennis Club; he was pondering a few choices for the evening's entertainment. Gin rummy at the Kings X was a possibility, or shuffleboard at the Kerosene Club. The Kings X was about to get the nod when a member walked in and, out of the blue, offered Whitney a $100 to drive him to Reno in the morning. The guy was a friend, a Viet Nam veteran who smoked too much. Whitney checked his social calendar and said, "Oookay, I can do that." The next day, about 11 a.m., the vet, Whitney, and vet's Cadillac headed up I-80 to Reno.

They made it as far as Roseville before they needed to replenish their supply of beer. Whitney knew of a bar with a pool table that was on the way out of town. They stopped for a couple of games and then headed back up the mountain. Just pass the Auburn exit was a Hilton billboard that prominently displayed the smiling face of Bill Cosby.

The vet said, "Hey, I've never seen Bill Cosby in person; when we get to Reno, plot a course for the Hilton Hotel."

Whitney said, "Allllright, I kind of know Bill. I was living up here with a lady who served cocktails on the second floor of Harold's Club. Claudia, but that's another story. I played a lot of tennis with Bill, sooo I know him pretty well. I was teaching tennis at the Y in the summer and driving a cab in the winter – you know." (If you have a chance to converse with Whitney, listen closely)

Whitney pulled the Cadillac up to the valet parking area and took a ticket from the attendant. In the intervening 10 seconds, the vet was out the car door and into the casino.

By the time Whitney had pocketed the valet ticket and walked into the casino the vet had lost all his money, and when Whitney found him standing next to a crap table, the first thing he said was, "Whitney, can I have the hundred back?"

Whitney sat at the bar thinking, "What the fuck do I do now." He was out of money, the member was surely out of money, and it was about zero degrees outside. He knew Bill Cosby was somewhere in the hotel, but he hated to exploit an old friendship. Cosby was an avid tennis player, and he and

Whitney had played in a few celebrity tournaments together. But putting the arm on a celebrity, or anyone for that matter, was very distasteful to Whitney. He prided himself on his self-reliance. The tougher the situation, the more of a challenge it was to survive. The problem was the situation was approaching a critical juncture; it was either face Harrah's security team, freeze, or call Cosby. He was about to make a decision when the vet slid onto the next stool. Too say that he was in shock was an understatement; he was in all-out panic mode.

(I recorded this story at lunch on June 12, 2005)

"Sooo now you can imagine, it's 9'oclock in the evening and we have no money," said Whitney. "Oooooh, what was there to do? I've got to go to the desk and call Bill. Well, low and behold, Bill Cosby answers the phone."

Whitney says, "Hello Bill this is…"

Bill Cosby says, "I know who it is."

"Well, Bill, aaaah, you won't believe what happened, we've only been here 20 minutes and we lost all our money. This fellow hired me and…"

"Yes, Whitney," says Bill Cosby.

"Well, aaaah, Bill, could you, could you comp us a room for the evening?"

There was a long silence

"All right Whitney, but please don't let this happen again."

"Thank you, Bill."

When the check came for lunch, I asked Whitney how they got down the mountain. Whitney, once again, said that they must have coasted.

- CHAPTER 36 -

More Bill Cosby

Whitney got a big bang out of playing with Bill Cosby. He enjoyed Bill's competitive nature, and the incongruity of a celebrity who would almost rather win on a tennis court than win an Oscar.

According to Whitney, Cosby was one competitive dude. When Whitney played in celebrity events he'd keep the ball in play, and let everyone have a chance to take a whack at it. Not so with Bill, who was out to win. If Whitney danced around the ball, doing his Charlie Chaplin imitation of a tennis player, Cosby would scream, "Goddamit, Whitney, put the mother-fucking ball away."

In Monte Carlo, Bill would stay on his boat rather then join the celebrity festivities. He was out to win and replace Robert Duval as the No. 1 celebrity tennis player. Consequently, when Whitney played with Cosby he put out a little more effort into the game. It was either play a little harder or get used to Cosby's Pancho Gonzalez bad eye, and one Pancho in Whitney's life was enough.

Whitney ended the Bill Cosby soliloquy with an affectionate comment, "Bless his heart, Bill's a good boy and he did give us a bed for the night."

- CHAPTER 37 -

Unsaintly Issues
You Shouldn't Share
With Your Mother

Alameda High School has to be the kissing school on the planet. All anyone ever talked about was kissing. Making out, smash mouth, sucking face, Alameda kids had more colloquialisms for the male of the species placing his lips on the female of the species then mud on the mudflats. It must be the weather; Alameda is so cold that kids needed to make out just to stay warm. The fog would roll in off the bay and the streets would empty, not a high school kid in sight. Everyone would race to their cars, drive out to the mud flats, and start kissing like crazy. The only virgins in the town were the kids without cars.

There's always a first time for everything: first kiss, first cigarette, first can of beer, and the first time you get drunk and barf your guts out. Whitney has been kissing girls, drinking beer, and smoking cigarettes for as long as he can remember. Nevertheless, the fact that he's been doing these dreadful things for so long did not preclude his current squeeze from quizzing him on a few past carnal occurrences – as in, "Hey, Whitney, when was the first time you got laid?"

For most people, a question of such a personal nature is a bit perplexing, but not for Whitney. He had no problem in articulating the details in a candid and graphic manner.

He was 18 years old. A virgin in Alameda who has reached his or her 18th birthday is a rarity. As rare as finding a flock of Dodo birds on the mud flats, as rare as finding an alligator in the estuary, and as rare as a white point guard at Encinal High. When I was a student at Alameda High, and that was in the late 1950s, one needed to be very careful when opening a door that was not at least half glass; any utility closet, janitor's storage area, or any space that could accommodate two bodies was approached with extreme caution. Consequently, as a virgin, 18-year-old Whitney Reed was a huge absurdity.

Even more confounding, Whitney had been playing tennis on the junior circuit since he was 12. There was a ton of cute willing girls at every tournament, and there are always dances, parties, hotel rooms – millions of opportunities to lose one's virginity.

Even more of an incongruity, Whitney did not lose his virginity with some cute little Alameda girl who lived on the gold coast. He didn't pursue a long- legged sweetie from Mr. Coughlin's chemistry class, or engage in some witty repartee with a good-looking hall monitor. He didn't try and charm some little nymphet with a movie at the Alameda Theatre, followed by hot apple pie at Mel's in Oakland. Nope, not Whitney, nothing traditional, no kissy-face foreplay in the parlor of an Alameda Victorian, or fogging the windows of a '39 Chevy with four on the floor. Whitney's sojourn into life's mysteries had to be spectacular.

Spectacular it was: He and a buddy drove to Sacramento on a hot Friday afternoon. They found a joint called Jack's in West Sacramento. Jack's featured a hooker who went by the name of Toy.

Whitney and his buddy drove back from Sacramento that hot Friday afternoon, neither of them paying much attention to the heat. In fact, it could have been 100 degrees or 20 degrees; all they knew was that they had finally achieved non-virgin status.

Annie may have had a clue

Norm Peterson and Whitney were formidable doubles partners. They played doubles in high school and never lost a match. That in itself was no feat, but they beat Ham Richardson and Jack Frost in the 18-year-old finals at Kalamazoo, Michigan, and that win was a feat.

In 1955, Norm and Whitney topped their win in Kalamazoo by beating Herbie Flam and Art Larsen in the Pacific Coast Championships at the Berkeley Tennis Club. An incredible feat: Art Larsen was the No. 3 player in the world and Herbie Flam was no slouch. I think of that win in terms of Pete Pinto and I beating Cheney and Neeley, something that would occur about the time the Dodo birds renew their acquaintance with the Alameda mudflats.

What Annie may or may not have known about Kalamazoo in 1950 was that Norm and Whitney played second-story men the night before the finals. Surreptitiously, they scooted out an upper floor window and made their way to a party that included a couple of the more adventurous local girls. They must have had a great time because neither Whitney nor Norm will divulge much of the evening's events. They just smile that smile that says, "Oh, to be young again." What we do know is that Kalamazoo occurred after Whitney's trip to Sacramento and the infamous Toy.

Whitney was never sure what Annie knew and what she didn't know. Through the years and especially the last five, Annie would mention an event that would stop Whitney in his tracks. Like the time during their nightly gin game when, out of the blue, she asked Whitney what he and Norm Peterson did that night in 1950 when they played second-story men.

- CHAPTER 38 -

Life After Annie –
June 19, 2005 and Forward

Claudia flew out from Houston to help Whitney put Annie's estate in order. She marched into the little house in Alameda and took command. She tore into closets and storage areas that Annie hadn't touched in years. Piles of cloths, hats, trophies, and shoes were strewn everywhere. Whitney was relegated to a small area in front of the TV set. Claudia immediately formed a plan for Whitney's future: The little house must be remodeled.

She enlisted the help of Whitney's family in planning a memorial. The event was at Pier 29 in Alameda. Whitney rented the conference area and popped for the booze and food. The room was decorated with Annie's pictures and trophies. In the center of the room against the east wall was a huge bouquet of flowers. The tables were in a U-shape with Whitney and Claudia at the head table. Ed Atkinson and I were seated on one side of the U, and little kids were scattered everywhere. Across from Ed and me sat Matt and Ed Murphy. They had been friends of Whitney and Annie for years. Ed actually taught tennis in Alameda on his own private court. The rest of the room was strewn hither and yon with family, plus Don Coughlin and his physician girlfriend, and Seth Peterson and his wife.

Whitney and Ed Atkinson were in marginal shape for the memorial. They went out to dinner the night before and made it home by 12:30 a.m. – a shadow of a performance when compared to the good old days.

Pier 29, just over the Park Street Bridge from Alameda, is a hangout for everyone from local judges to local drunks. The food is good, the drinks generous, and it has a great view of the estuary. Sailboats move along the waterway, periodically forcing the bridges to open and traffic to stop. Whitney and Claudia decided on Pier 29 as the site for Annie's memorial.

Pier 29's bright conference room in the back of the main dining room is perfect for weddings, sales meetings, and Veterans of Foreign Wars assemblies. The room is not Art Deco, more 1950-ish neo-modern – quintessential Alameda. Alameda is so old fashioned. Once you cross the Park Street Bridge, you are in another world. It's like a piece of the Midwest. Anybody over 50 and a native of the town looks and acts as if he or she were auditioning for Our Town. Even the clerks at City Hall have a Dickensesque flavor, green shades on their heads and starched collars around their necks.

Whitney, from his perch at the head table, coughed and growled for everyone to take a seat. Once everyone was seated, Whitney proceeded to introduce the quests. He announced names, a brief biography, and their association with Annie. I've been to a thousand memorials, and this particular affair was very touching. It was like watching Judy Garland; charmed by the performance, but troubled by the frailty of the performer.

After lunch the guests milled around chatting and reminiscing about the good old days of wood racquets and all-white tennis attire.

Ed and Whitney looked particularly anxious. A few days later, when Whitney and I were on the way to a Giants game, he told me that he and Ed had made a quick sojourn to a local card room. He said that he had won a few bucks playing poker, and Ed had lost a couple of bucks – no damage just some good fun. Quite a contrast to times past, Ed and Whitney were home by midnight and asleep by 12:30, which must be the witching hour for people between the ages of 68 and 73.

- CHAPTER 39 -

The Hands Are Fine, the Legs Are Another Matter

I picked up Whitney at the Palm Springs airport in my Jeep wrangler. He was standing on the curb in black warm-up pants and a coffee stained tennis sweater from the early '60s.

"Heeey, nice Jeep ... Gooodamn the weather's nice ... haven't been to bed since yesterday ... but no matter, feel as fit as a fiddle,"

"Hi, sweetie, doesn't Whit look great ... we haven't been to bed yet," said his friend, Gail.

Being around Whitney for any length of time causes distinct damage to your communication skills. You start mixing metaphors, splitting infinitives, and taking extraordinary long pauses between sentences. After a while, if you are not careful, every time you open your mouth, it sounds like a stream of conscientiousness.

Gail, Whitney, and I folded ourselves into my Jeep and headed in the general direction of Palm Desert. Whitney brought a tennis bag and a duffel bag; Gail brought enough luggage to give the Jeep a distinct list. Our short trip to Palm Desert resembled the Joads crossing the Rio Grande on their way to California. Most of Gail's luggage was poking out in all directions. Whitney had a small valise in his lap and very large suitcase jabbing him in the back.

When I drove the Jeep into the driveway Whitney said, "Sooon of a bitch I'm tired ... need a little sleep ... only an hour or so ... be up and at 'em before you know it." Six hours later Whitney and I took off for the tennis courts.

Jackie Cooper and Lornie Kuhle leased the facilities at the Palm Desert Resort Country Club and spent about a zillion dollars beautifying the place. They are well on their way to making the "Resorter" the best tennis facility in the Coachella

Valley. Lornie has a ton of experience in owning and managing tennis clubs, and everyone loves Jackie. Lornie has an ongoing, successful relationship with Jimmy Connors, and was a life-long friend of Bobby Riggs. Jackie is a legend in the Valley. Lornie takes care of the money, and Jackie takes care of the charm – should be a formula for success. They've been open only a few months, the parking lot is full, and the sounds of tennis are reverberating around the "Resorter" once again.

Jackie Cooper and Whitney greeted one another like long-lost war buddies. They hugged and patted each other on the back the way sisters do; five minutes later, they're off in a cor-ner firing up a Marlboro. Old tennis players have many bad habits; they smoke, drink too much, and generally take very poor care of themselves. Jack Frost being an exception, he looks like he could fight a band saw.

Jackie grabbed a racquet and hustled Whitney out onto the tennis court. Whitney hitched up his black Prince warm-ups and whacked a forehand to Jackie's backhand. Jackie chipped a return to Whitney's forehand. Whitney hit a backhand drop shot that Jackie covered easily. Whitney bent over, leaned on his racquet and said, "Sooon of a bitch, I've got to get in bet-ter shape ... let's have a beer and play some backgammon."

Jack Darrrah showed up about mid-afternoon and wanted to play some doubles, so Jackie and Whitney played Jack and me. Jackie and Whitney won in a tiebreaker. Jackie hit about 1000 balls to Whitney's two; no matter, Whitney seemed to enjoy himself.

Jack Darrah is a super backgammon player, a player Whitney could almost never beat. Whitney said it was because Jack used to be a math teacher, and it gave him an unfair advantage. Jack could practice backgammon while all those poor kids were struggling over geometry problems. Jack and Whitney spent the afternoon huddled over a backgammon board, while everyone else watched Betty Ann Dent (Taylor Dent's mom) hit forehand volleys.

Dinner in the Resorter's dinning room was a trip. Jackie and Lornie were promoting the club, Whitney and Gail were dancing and generally entertaining everyone within earshot, and everyone else was drooling over Betty Ann.

The evening could have taken a turn for the worse. Lornie was watching Gail and Whitney like a hawk. Concern splashed all over his face; he was visualizing Whitney and Gail getting way too rowdy for the snowbird, Midwest crowd. The Midwest, slightly overweight, slightly right of center gang might not mesh with Whitney and Gail's far west, San Francisco liberal, "let's-dance-all-night" approach to life. The metaphor "sweating blood" comes to mind.

Just when Gail was about to perform her famous dance routine, sort of a spin, land on the floor, and splits step, Whitney needed a smoke break. The pause gave me just enough time to hustle Gail and Whitney out the door and into the Jeep. Away we went, Lornie was saved from a potentially embarrassing situation, Jackie was able to "slip out the back, Jack" and get home to his fiancée, and I was the most relieved of all – I was not stuck in the middle.

The paramount reason for Whitney's trip to Palm Desert, other then to give his lungs a break from the Alameda fog, was to help promote Jackie and Lornie's 100-year-old tennis tournament. (The ages of the doubles team must be 100 years or older) Originally, Jackie wanted to play with Whitney, but

Whitney was not in good enough shape to run around for an eight-game pro-set. Jackie teamed with Rosie Casals, and Whitney was elected coach.

The day of the finals was Super Bowl Sunday. The idea was to get the tournament over in time to watch the game. Jackie and Rosie lost to a couple of guys from Palm Springs. Rosie was berating Jackie every inch of the way. Jackie needed to move faster, try harder, and hit a bigger serve. Whitney, the coach, wanted Rosie to get to the net faster. Acrimony could have raised its ugly head with anyone but Jackie, Rosie, and Whitney. Rosie can be a little testy, but Jackie and Whitney, the world's easiest people to be around, kept the event in perspective.

Merv Griffin made a welcomed appearance. Lornie and Jackie set up an umbrella, and fussed over him like a couple of old women. As it should be, Merv is good for tennis. He loves the game, and promotes it at every opportunity.

When Merv spotted Whitney strolling along the walkway adjacent to the stadium court, he called him over and made him part and party to a quick smoke. At 80 years old, Merv figures, what the hell, age will get me before the smoke does.

He and Whitney chatted away like a couple of old war horses.

Jack and Helenka made an appearance and seemed to enjoy themselves. Gail was introduced to the Frosts – which could be compared to Auntie Mame bonding with Vanessa Redgrave. Gail was her delightfully, bubbly self. Helenka was, as always, charming and slightly reserved. Reserved in a fashion that she gives the impression that she knows a little bit more about life than the rest of us.

Knowing smart, sophisticated people is a unique challenge. They are tough to con, and they're too well bred to be openly

judgmental. Helenka and Jack are the epitome of sophistica-
tion, and they have tolerance, an element that all genuinely
sophisticated people possess. They know good manners from
bad; they know which fork goes with the salad; they know
verbs, adverbs, and modifiers. Knowing what's accepted in
polite society and what's accepted in a poolroom, they choose
to use "is not" rather than "ain't." Jack and Helenka choose
to be Whitney's friends, and that speaks volumes for Whitney's
value as a person and a personality.

- CHAPTER 40 -

The Final Curtain
and
Some Final
Shoddy Thoughts

Pancho Segura, holding court at Jackie Cooper's Tennis Center in Palm Desert, California, says Whitney is hard to be around. He's unpredictable; you never know what he is about to say. He may be the most charming person at a party, or he may suddenly take all his clothes off and jump into the pool. Pancho says Whitney could have been an even greater player if he trained. He said Whitney had the best half-volley in the business.

Pancho shakes his head and says, "but, man he's toooo scary to be around; you never know what he's going to pull. A real frightening guy."

Jackie Cooper, the great equalizer, jumped up, got in a deep crouch and mimicked Whitney's bolo half-volley and said, "Whitney would skid the ball into either corner, and if you were lucky enough to get it back he'd charge the net like a gorilla, and slap a volley to any spot on the court."

Everyone laughed, obviating Pancho's biting remarks. I'm definitely losing journalistic perspective; I found myself getting pissed at an 85-year-old tennis legend. The time I've spent getting to know Whitney has made me a bit too protective.

Pancho's cool, and he has his right to an opinion. He has definitely paid his dues, and at 85 he's as sharp as a tack. When I'm 85, I only hope I can go to the bathroom by myself, let alone participate in a tennis discussion with a bunch of tennis players half my age.

Pancho is nine years older than Whitney, and seven inches shorter. Pancho had to fight his way from Ecuador to Miami to even get a chance to play major league tennis. Whitney had to fight his way from Third Street in Alameda to Washington Park, a distance about as far as Frank Robinson can hit a baseball. When Pancho turned pro in 1946, Whitney was jumping out of the window at the Asilomar in Carmel. When Pancho was playing competitively against, Riggs, Kramer, and Gonzalez, Whitney was playing competitively against Frost, Richardson, and Norm Peterson.

Pancho had to work so hard to possess the best forehand of his era. Whitney's mid-court game just happened from conception. Pancho had to conquer a myriad of physical shortcomings to achieve success. All Whitney had to overcome was avoiding an extra Martini at a pre-match party. Pancho looks at Whitney and thinks: If I had that natural ability I'd be the best in the world and maybe the best ever. Whitney looks at Pancho and says in Whitney talk, "That feisty little shit was a hell of a tennis player."

If we are not planning on hitting a few balls, a typical Whitney day may include fixing the coffee, reading the Chronicle, and skipping down to the Lemon Tree where he'll nurse a short screwdriver for about a week and a half. (Rumors of Whitney's reputation as a drinker have been greatly exaggerated, and sightings of a drunken Whitney are about as rare as the NBA playoffs are for the Warriors) If we are planning on hitting a few balls then the day is a little different, I watch Whitney drink a little coffee, read the Chronicle. We hit for a while then go to the Lemon Tree.

Tommy Tucker said it best of all, "I'm not interested in discussing Whitney's shortcomings, he's too much of a personality, and he has too much to offer. Dwelling on wine and women does not do justice to the man any more than dwelling on gambling does justice to Bobby Riggs."

In the not to distant past, cloistered would be a safe description of Whitney's life---cloistered and terminally boring. He would spend his days playing gin rummy, and working the New York Times crossword puzzles. In the not to distant future, chances were pretty good that some day someone will knock on his door, find it open, and Whitney will be sitting on the sofa in front of the television watching reruns of "Cheyenne." The Whitney on the sofa, the one who fought Rafael Osuna to a stand still, will be in physical form only; his spirit will have already joined Vines, Kovacs, and Riggs.

Ain't going to happen folks, because I know what's going to happen. He'll play another tournament ---count on it. He'll play even if he needs courtside oxygen. I can see him running down a crosscourt forehand, stopping for a quick shot of oxygen, and winning another gold ball. Imagine a Chronicle Sports Section headline: Whitney Reed wins the (?) Senior Nationals played at Jackie Cooper's Tennis Center in Palm Desert, California. Not that farfetched if you know Whitney Reed. Maybe he can get Jack Frost to play doubles with him. Imagine the Monterey flash, and the Alameda splash together again.

His health is improving, and he seems to have his mother's constitution; he could possibly survive another 10 years. He is not rich, but with careful planning, money shouldn't be a concern. All he really needs is what he already possesses: great memories and few regrets

Whitney's legacy is not about performing unmentionable atrocities, either on or off the tennis court. Whitney is not about gin rummy, backgammon, and booze. Whitney is not about jumping nude into a swimming pool. Whitney is about forehands and backhands, half-volley lobs, and drop shots. He is about great drama, great theater, and more than a little pathos. Whitney is to tennis what Robards was to Broadway, or what Pavarotti was to La Scala. Too bad, and so wretched for tennis, he is one of a kind and sadly, the last of a kind.